brilliant

Microsoft®
Word
2007

POCKET BOOK

Deanna Reynolds

Harlow, England • London • New York • Boston • San Francisco • Toronto
Sydney • Tokyo • Singapore • Hong Kong • Seoul • Taipei • New Delhi
Cape Town • Madrid • Mexico City • Amsterdam • Munich • Paris • Milan

Pearson Education Limited
Edinburgh Gate
Harlow CM20 2JE
Tel: +44 (0)1279 623623
Fax: +44 (0)1279 431059
Website: www.pearsoned.co.uk

First published in Great Britain in 2007

@ Joli Ballew 2007

The right of Deanna Reynolds to be identified as author of this work has been asserted by
her in accordance with the Copyright, Designs and Patents Act 1988.

ISBN: 978-0-132-05970-1

British Library Cataloguing-in-Publication Data
A catalogue record for this book is available from the British Library

Microsoft product screen shots reprinted with permission from Microsoft Corporation.

10 9 8 7 6 5 4 3 2 1
11 10 09 08 07

Typeset in 10pt Helvetica by 3
Printed and bound in Great Britain by Ashford Colour Press Ltd., Gosport

The Publisher's policy is to use paper manufactured from sustainable forests.

Brilliant Pocket Books

What you need to know – when you need it!

When you're working on your PC and come up against a problem that you're unsure how to solve, or want to accomplish something in an application that you aren't sure how to do, where do you look? If you are fed up with wading through pages of background information in unwieldy manuals and training guides trying to find the piece of information or advice that you need RIGHT NOW, and if you find that helplines really aren't that helpful, then Brilliant Pocket Books are the answer!

Brilliant Pocket Books have been developed to allow you to find the info that you need easily and without fuss and to guide you through each task using a highly visual step-by-step approach – providing exactly what you need to know, when you need it!

Brilliant Pocket Books are concise, easy-to-access guides to all of the most common important and useful tasks in all of the applications in the Office 2007 suite. Short, concise lessons make it really easy to learn any particular feature, or master any task or problem that you will come across in day-to-day use of the applications.

When you are faced with any task on your PC, whether major or minor, that you are unsure about, your Brilliant Pocket Book will provide you with the answer – almost before you know what the question is!

Brilliant Pocket Books Series

Series Editor: Joli Ballew

Brilliant Microsoft® Access 2007 Pocket Book	*S.E. Slack*
Brilliant Microsoft® Excel 2007 Pocket Book	*J. Peter Bruzzese*
Brilliant Microsoft® Office 2007 Pocket Book	*Jerri Ledford & Rebecca Freshour*
Brilliant Microsoft® Outlook 2007 Pocket Book	*Meryl K. Evans*
Brilliant Microsoft® PowerPoint 2007 Pocket Book	*S.E. Slack*
Brilliant Microsoft® Windows Vista 2007 Pocket Book	*Jerri Ledford & Rebecca Freshour*
Brilliant Microsoft® Word 2007 Pocket Book	*Deanna Reynolds*

Contents

Introduction

Welcome to the *Brilliant Microsoft® Word 2007 Pocket Book* – a handy visual quick reference that will give you a basic grounding in the common features and tasks that you will need to master to use Microsoft® Word 2007 in any day-to-day situation. Keep it on your desk, in your briefcase or bag – or even in your pocket! – and you will always have the answer to hand for any problem or task that you come across.

Find out what you need to know – when you need it!

You don't have to read this book in any particular order. It is designed so that you can jump in, get the information you need and jump out – just look up the task in the contents list, turn to the right page, read the introduction, follow the step-by-step instructions – and you're done!

How this book works

Each section in this book includes foolproof step-by-step instructions for performing specific tasks, using screenshots to illustrate each step. Additional information is included to help increase your understanding and develop your skills – these are identified by the following icons:

 Jargon buster – New or unfamiliar terms are defined and explained in plain English to help you as you work through a section.

 Timesaver tip – These tips give you ideas that cut corners and confusion. They also give you additional information related to the topic that you are currently learning. Use them to expand your knowledge of a particular feature or concept.

 Important – This identifies areas where new users often run into trouble, and offers practical hints and solutions to these problems.

Brilliant Pocket Books are a handy, accessible resource that you will find yourself turning to time and time again when you are faced with a problem or an unfamiliar task and need an answer at your fingertips – or in your pocket!

1

Familiarising Yourself with Word

Microsoft Word 2007 is a greatly improved version of the word-processing program that Microsoft has made available for years. This application provides you with all of the tools that you need to create documents such as letters, faxes, newsletters, reports and calendars. And now, with Word 2007, creating these documents as well as more graphic-intense documents such as certificates and flyers has just become easier. Plus, if you're really adventurous, you can even create web pages.

In fact, with Word 2007, word processing isn't just about typing letters any more. Word processing has evolved to a level that no longer requires the average user to be an experienced graphic designer to be able to produce amazing documents.

→ Opening Word

Before you can even think about creating your first Word document, you have to start the application. There are a couple of ways to launch (*or open*) the Word program, but let's first look at the most common ones.

With Windows Vista, you can access Word (*and other installed programs*) by clicking the Start button. To start Word using the **Start** button, follow these steps:

1 Beginning from the Windows Vista desktop, click the **Start** button in the lower left corner of the page. As shown in Figure 1.1, the **Start Menu** appears.

Figure 1.1
Click the Start button to access the Start menu and the All Programs option.

2 Select **All Programs** and then click the **Microsoft Office** folder. The Microsoft Office folder expands to show the icons representing the different Office programs.

3 Click the **Microsoft Office Word 2007** link and Microsoft
Word will open to a blank page.

Once you have opened Word on at least one occasion, a
shortcut to the Word program will probably appear on your **Start
menu** the next time you click the Start button. If this happens,
you can open your Word program from the **Start menu** following
these steps:

1 Beginning from the Windows Vista desktop, click the **Start**
button in the lower left corner of the page. The **Start menu**
expands.

2 From the **Start menu** click **Microsoft Office Word 2007**.
Microsoft Word will open to a blank page.

One fact you should note about using this second method to
open Word is that the Start menu changes according to the
programs that you use most often. When you open one program,
it can replace another program that appears on the Start menu.
However, you can "pin" an item to the Start menu – effectively
making the "pinned" link available each time you view the Start
menu. For example, most computers are set up to display an
Internet link and an e-mail link at the top of the Start menu. When
you "pin" a program shortcut, such as Microsoft Office Word
2007, to the Start menu, it appears near the top of the Start
menu with the Internet and e-mail links.

To pin Microsoft Word to the Start menu, follow these steps:

1 Click the **Start** button and navigate to the **Microsoft Office
Word 2007** icon.

2 Right-click on the icon and then, as shown in Figure 1.2,
select **Pin to Start Menu.** The Word icon will then
be permanently fixed to the Start menu until you
"unpin" it.

Regardless of the method you choose to open Word 2007, each
time the program is opened, you're greeted with a new, blank
document.

Figure 1.2
Select "Pin to Start Menu" to affix the Word icon to the Start menu.

→ Using the Word Ribbon

One of the major differences that you'll notice immediately in Word 2007 is the change in the navigational structure of the program. Part of a new results-oriented user interface, where once you saw dropdown menus you'll now see the **Ribbon**, as shown in Figure 1.3.

Figure 1.3
The Ribbon is designed to make accomplishing tasks in Word faster and easier.

Timesaver tip

The **Ribbon** is the configuration of tabs and command buttons across the top of the screen in Word 2007. All of the commands that were once buried in menus can be found on the Ribbon, and contextual tabs appear and disappear according to the tasks you are performing.

The Ribbon, while a little daunting at first glance, is designed to make it faster and easier for you to accomplish any of your tasks in Word. Instead of digging through menu after menu to find the function or capability that you need, now all you have to do is look at the commands on the Ribbon.

By default, the Word Ribbon is divided into seven tabs (see "Default Ribbon Tabs"). Many of the new tabs closely mimic a menu found in previous versions of Word.

Jargon buster

Contextual tabs are the new menus for Word 2007. These tabs typically represent menus from previous versions of the program and group together similar capabilities. With visual representation for every command, they allow you to quickly see the commands available in each group.

The Word 2007 Ribbon tabs group together sets of similar capabilities. In addition to the default seven, there are other tabs, as shown in Figure 1.4, that appear only when you need them. These contextual tabs simply appear as you're working. For example, the **Pictures Tools Format** tab appears only when you have selected an image you have already inserted into your document.

Figure 1.4
Contextual tabs put all of the functionality of Word at your fingertips, but appear only when you need them.

Default Ribbon Tabs

While there are several contextual tabs that appear when you're working with advanced functions such as tables, charts and images, there are seven default tabs that are always available when working on a Word document. These tabs are arranged according to the functions that you use most frequently in Word and contain buttons for everything you'll need to do in Word (*aside from basic file management commands that were once found on the File menu*).

- **Home**: The Home tab contains the functions that you'll use most often when working with a document, including cut, copy and paste. The Home tab has been divided into five logical groups: Clipboard, Font, Paragraph, Styles and Editing.

- **Insert**: The functions on the Insert tab allow you to add elements to your documents. There are seven distinct groups on the Insert tab: Pages, Tables, Illustrations, Links, Header and Footer, Text and Symbols.

- **Page Layout**: The Page Layout tab is where you'll find the functions that let you arrange your document pages in the most useful manner. The five groups of commands are: Themes, Page Setup, Page Background, Paragraph and Arrange.

- **References**: The References tab is where you'll find some of the functions that you might have had difficulty locating in the past. These functions enable you to quickly and easily add elements of depth to your documents, particularly when working with long documents. The References tab has been divided into six groups: Table of Contents, Footnotes, Citations & Bibliography, Captions, Index and Table of Authorities.

- **Mailings**: The Mailings tab is where you'll find all the commands you'll need when working with labels, envelopes and mail merge documents. Listed in logical order based on the mail merge process, the groups found on the Mailings tab are: Create, Start Mail Merge, Write & Insert Fields, Preview Results and Finish.

- **Review**: In addition to proofing, you'll find commands related to the editing process and sharing files on the Review tab. With six groups, you'll find commands on the Review tab organised by: Proofing, Comments, Tracking, Changes, Compare and Protect.

- **View**: The old View menu is essentially now the new View tab. With the commands found on the View tab, you have additional control over how your document appears on your screen as you're working on it. On the View tab you'll find five groups: Document Views, Show/Hide, Zoom, Window and Macros.

One more trick with the Ribbon. If you find that it's awkward for you to have the Ribbon visible all the time, you can hide it temporarily. To hide or restore the Ribbon, follow these steps:

1 Right-click anywhere on the Ribbon. A pop-up menu appears.

2 Click **Minimize the Ribbon** to hide it. The tabs will remain visible. Once the Ribbon is hidden, you can make it temporarily reappear by clicking on any tab. If you display the Ribbon, clicking anywhere inside your document will hide it again.

3 To restore the Ribbon, right-click on any tab and deselect **Minimize the Ribbon**. The Ribbon will be restored to its original position at the top of the document.

In addition to the Ribbon, there are a few other controls with which you should be familiar. As Figure 1.5 shows, the File menu now appears in the upper left corner of the Word screen as the Office button. When you click this button, the familiar File menu appears.

On the Office menu, there are recognisable options such as New, Open, Save and Save As. You'll also find options here for Print, Prepare, Send, Publish, Close, Word Options and Exit Word.

Figure 1.5
The File menu is now located behind the Office button.

One more useful element of Word 2007 is the **Quick Access toolbar**, shown in Figure 1.6.

1

Jargon buster

The **Quick Access toolbar** is located at the top of your screen. It contains the most frequently used commands from the Ribbon and tabs in Word. You can add or remove any Word command to customise this toolbar.

The Quick Access toolbar initially offers you quick access to some of the most common functions (*such as Save, Undo and Redo*) that you'll use most often when working in Word. This toolbar puts those options a single click away instead of burying them under the Office Menu or on a tab on the Ribbon.

Figure 1.6
The Quick Access toolbar puts the most common functions right on your screen for one-click access.

→ Changing Your View

The way you view documents in Microsoft Word is a matter of personal choice. Some people like to use print layout, while others like to use web layout. There are even a few who like the draft view. Each of these layouts offers its own unique benefits. What's nice is the option to choose the layout that works best based on the document type you're working on.

Using the Document Display

In Word 2007, you have the option of using the View tab to change the way you view your document. Additionally, there is a View toolbar in the lower right corner of the Word screen, as shown in Figure 1.7. This toolbar gives you five viewing options: Print Layout, Full Screen Reading, Web Layout, Outline and Draft. To use the View toolbar to switch between these layouts, simply left-click the desired layout. This way, you can always return to your desired view by clicking the associated layout button either on the View tab in the Ribbon or on the View toolbar.

Figure 1.7
The layout buttons allow you to quickly switch between document views.

Zooming in on Your Document

Next to the Layout buttons, Word 2007 displays a brand-new **Zoom Slider**. This allows you to quickly see your document at different size ratios.

Jargon buster

The **Zoom Slider** allows you to quickly change the size ratio of your document. You can rapidly zoom in or out of a document by sliding the control either left (out) or right (in).

To change the size ratio of the document in which you are working, click and drag the **Zoom** control button on the **Zoom Slider**. Using this control, you can change the size of your document from 10% of the original to 500%. To see the entire page, this is a much faster alternative to viewing the document in Print Preview.

Using the Document Map

The **document map**, shown in Figure 1.8, is basically an interactive outline of your document.

Jargon buster

The **document map** is an interactive outline of your document that allows you to quickly move from one heading to another.

To access the document map, click the **View** tab and then place a checkmark in the box next to **Document Map** located in the **Show/Hide** group on the Ribbon.

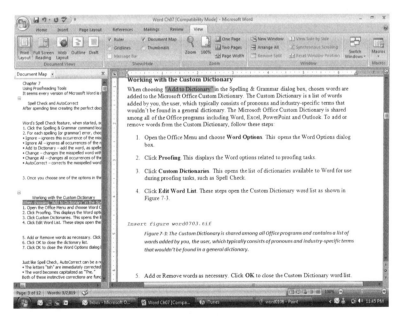

Figure 1.8
The document map is an interactive outline of the current document. Clicking headings in the map will take you to that heading in the document.

The document map is most useful in documents that are very long and use the built-in heading styles (Heading 1, Heading 2, etc.). Instead of having to scroll through pages and pages of text to find what you're looking for, you can open the document map and select the heading you want to jump to. You'll be taken to that heading in the document immediately.

Comparing Documents Side by Side

Sometimes, it's far more effective if you can view two documents side by side. This capability might be used to compare versions of a document or to compare information in two different documents. Follow these steps:

1 Open the two documents that you would like to compare.

2 In one document, click the **View** tab.

3 From the **Window** section of the tab, select **View Side by Side.**

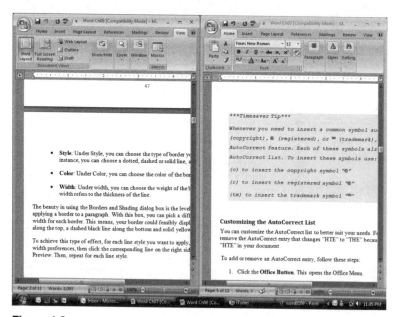

Figure 1.9
The Side-by-Side view allows you to compare two documents side by side.

4 As Figure 1.9 shows, the two documents will be placed side by side on your display.

5 When you've finished viewing your documents side by side, you can return to your original document view by clicking the **Maximize** button.

→ Saving Documents and Closing Word

After you have worked with a document in Word 2007, you will probably want to save it to come back to at a later time. Saving documents in Word is easy:

1 From the open document, click the **Office Menu button** located in the upper left corner.

2 From the menu that appears, click **Save.**

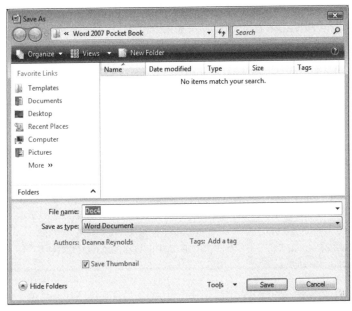

Figure 1.10
Use the Save As dialogue box to select the location to which the file will be saved and to add a file name.

3 The **Save As** dialogue box will appear, as shown in Figure 1.10.

4 Enter a name for the document in the **File Name** text box, select the location to which you would like to save the file and then click the **Save** button. The file will be saved to your chosen location.

With this method documents will automatically be saved as Word 2007 files, which are different from files for previous Word versions. Files saved in the Word 2007 format are not compatible with older versions of Microsoft Word. Therefore, there may be times when you need to save a file in a format that is compatible with a previous version of Word. You can do this by following these steps:

1 From the open document, click the **Office Menu button.**

2 From the menu that appears, select **Save As.**

3 Another menu appears. Select **Word 97-2003 Document**.

4 The **Save As** dialogue box appears.

5 Type a name for the document in the **File Name** box, select the location that you want the file saved to and click the **Save** button. The document will be saved to the selected location.

Timesaver tip

Once you've saved a file, you don't have to go through all of the above steps to save it incrementally. There are two ways to "quick save" your document: you can either click the **Save** icon in the **Quick Access** toolbar or you can use the keyboard shortcut combination **Ctrl+S**.

When you close Word, the program will also automatically prompt you to save your file if it was changed before closing, whether you've already given the document a name or not. To close Word, click the red **X** in the upper right corner of the program screen. As Figure 1.11 shows, if the document has not been saved, a prompt appears asking whether you want to save the document.

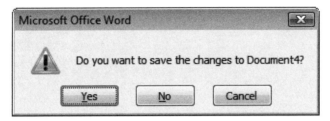

Figure 1.11
You are prompted to save your document before it closes.

If you choose **Yes**, the **Save As** dialogue box appears and you can proceed to save the file as directed above. If you choose **No**, all of the changes you've made to the document will be lost. If you select **Cancel**, you'll be returned to the document, which will remain open.

You can also close Word from the **Office Menu**:

1 Click the **Office Menu** button.

2 Select **Exit Word.**

3 A dialogue box appears prompting you to save your document, as explained above.

→ Summary

Navigating Word 2007 is a little different from previous versions of Word. It might take you some time to become comfortable with the Ribbon and the different views available for your documents. However, once you're comfortable moving around, you'll find it's easy to save and close your files.

In Chapter 2, you'll learn how to customise the Word program. The ability to change Word's appearance and customise the

Ribbon and the Quick Access toolbar gives you more control over Word than has ever been available in the past. This allows you to make the Word program work for you instead of the other way around.

2

Customising Word

One wish that's been high on the top of Word users' lists for quite some time is the ability to customise the Word environment to their tastes and work habits. In the past, there were some customisation features available, but Word 2007 brings a whole new set of customisation capabilities to the forefront.

→ Customising Word's Appearance

Looks aren't everything, but in Word 2007 they might as well be. With the redesigned user interface, Word users everywhere are trying to locate once favourite commands. We keep hearing Word's new look is really for our benefit but in the beginning it can be difficult to see those benefits as we struggle to locate our once familiar commands and functions.

Customise How Word Looks

One very cool feature of Word 2007 is the ability to customise the way that Word looks. Looks are not always about functionality. However, the way a program looks when you're using it can affect your productivity. Applications that are too stark or too glitzy can distract from your work flow. Unfortunately, what works for one person doesn't always work for another. Our application tastes can be as varied as our hair colour.

In Word 2007, you can customise your background style according to your personal preferences. To customise Word's look, use these steps:

1 Open a Word document. A blank document will be fine, but you can use a document that you've already begun working on, too.

2 Click the **Office button** in the top left corner of the page and select the **Word Options** button on the bottom of the menu that appears.

3 As Figure 2.1 shows, the **Word Options** dialogue box appears.

4 On the **Popular** screen (the default screen that appears in the Word Options dialogue box), click the **Color Scheme** dropdown menu.

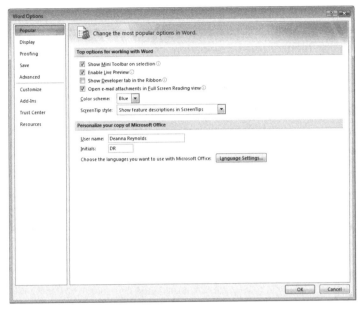

Figure 2.1
The Word Options dialogue box is where you can customise the appearance and behaviour of your Word program.

5 Select the desired colour from the available options and click **OK.** The colour scheme of your Word program will change to the one you have selected.

Customise How Word Acts

In addition to changing the background colour of Word, there are some customisation options available on the **Popular** screen that allow you to change how Word acts.

Working with the Custom Dic

When choosing "Add to Dictionary" in the Spelling & Grammar dialog added to the Microsoft Office Custom Dictionary. The Custom Diction added by you, the user, which typically consists of pronouns and indust

Figure 2.2
The Mini Toolbar is an in-context toolbar that appears only when you have highlighted some text.

One particular capability is how the **Mini toolbar** appears on your screen. The Mini Toolbar is an in-context toolbar that appears when you highlight a text selection, as shown in Figure 2.2.

This toolbar appears briefly only when you highlight text and it appears only very lightly. If you move your cursor towards the toolbar, it will brighten. If you move your cursor away from the toolbar, it will become more and more transparent until it disappears. Once the toolbar disappears, it will not return until you highlight more text.

Jargon buster

The **Mini Toolbar** is a contextual toolbar that appears only when you highlight some text. The toolbar is translucent on appearance and will brighten only if you move your pointer towards it. If you move your cursor away, the toolbar disappears and will not return until you select more text.

By default, the Mini Toolbar contains these buttons:

- Font
- Font Size
- Increase Text Size
- Decrease Text Size
- Text Style
- Format Painter
- Bold
- Italics
- Alignment
- Highlight
- Font Color
- Increase Indent

- Decrease Indent

- Bulleted Lists

You cannot change the tools that are available on the Mini Toolbar; however, you can turn it on and off. To change whether the Mini Toolbar appears when you highlight text, follow these steps:

1 Open a Word document. The document can be blank or it can be a document you have already created.

2 Click the **Office Menu** in the upper left corner of the page.

3 From the **Office Menu** that appears, select **Word Options** in the lower right corner of the menu.

4 The **Word Options** dialogue box appears. Select or deselect **Show Mini Toolbar on selection.** If you select the option, the Mini Toolbar will appear when you highlight text. If you deselect the option, it will not.

One other option that's available on the **Popular** screen is the ability to turn **Live Preview** on and off.

Jargon buster

Live Preview is a capability that allows you to see how changes to styles, themes and fonts will look in your document before you commit to them.

Live Preview is a new capability in Word 2007 that allows you to see how changes to styles, themes and fonts will look in your document before you commit to them. To see an example of Live Preview in action, follow these steps:

1 Open an existing document.

2 Place your cursor anywhere within the text.

3 On the **Home tab**, click **Change Styles** and select **Style Set.**

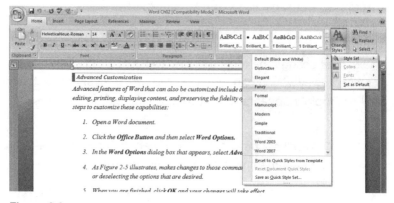

Figure 2.3
Placing your mouse pointer over any of the styles in the list will enable a live preview of that style within your document.

4 Place your mouse pointer over any of the styles in the list that appears and watch your document change to reflect that style, as shown in Figure 2.3.

5 The style of the selected text will change temporarily. To make the change permanent, click the selected style. The change will affect your selected text and you will be returned to your previous document view with the new style in effect.

→ Customising the Quick Access Toolbar

The Quick Access Toolbar is the small toolbar located in the upper left corner, next to the Office Button. This toolbar gives you the ability to quickly select the options that you use most often without having to move between tabs. It's a great place to put commands that you use frequently.

By default, the Quick Access Toolbar contains three buttons: Save, Undo and Redo. However, you can add any Word command to this toolbar.

There are two ways to customise your Quick Access Toolbar: from the **Word Options** menu or from the toolbar itself.

To customise the Quick Access Toolbar from the **Word Options** menu, follow these steps:

1 Open a Word document.

2 Click the **Office Menu**.

3 Select **Word Options** from the menu that appears.

4 In the **Word Options** dialogue box, select **Customize** from the menu on the left.

5 You are taken to the customisation page for the **Quick Access Toolbar** and keyboard shortcuts.

6 Using the **Choose commands from** dropdown menu, select the tab or location of the command you want to add to the Quick Access Toolbar. Figure 2.4 illustrates the tabs available.

7 The commands for that tab or area of Word will appear in

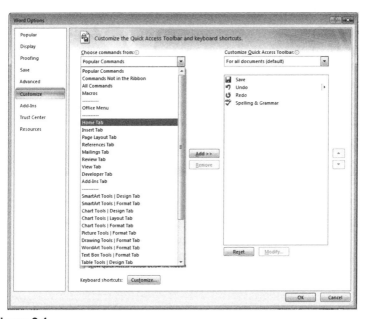

Figure 2.4
You can add any command from any tab or other location to the Quick Access Toolbar.

the dialogue box. Highlight the command you want to add to the Quick Access Toolbar and click **Add.**

8 The command will be added to the Quick Access Toolbar. You can rearrange the order in which the commands appear on the toolbar by using the up and down arrows to the right of the box that shows existing Quick Access commands.

9 To remove a command from the Quick Access Toolbar, highlight the command and click the **Remove** button.

10 You can also move the Quick Access Toolbar below the Ribbon by placing a check mark in the box next to **Show Quick Access Toolbar below the Ribbon.**

11 When you have finished customising the toolbar, click **OK** and the configurations that you've made will take effect.

Timesaver tip

You can also add and remove buttons on the **Quick Access Toolbar** from the **Quick Access Toolbar** menu. Click the downward arrow on the right end of the Quick Access Toolbar and select or deselect the commands that you want included on or removed from the Quick Access Toolbar.

→ Advanced Customisation

Advanced features of Word that can also be customised include document functionality such as editing, printing, displaying content and preserving the fidelity of a document. Follow these steps to customise these capabilities:

1 Open a Word document.

2 Click the **Office Menu** and then select **Word Options.**

3 In the **Word Options** dialogue box that appears, select **Advanced** from the menu on the left.

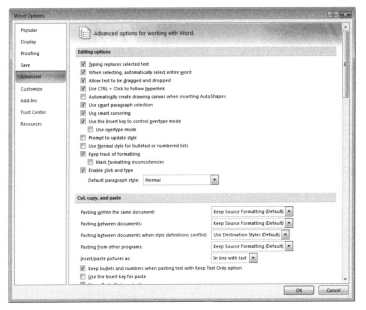

Figure 2.5
You can further customise the Word 2007 environment by selecting
(or deselecting) commands found under the Advanced category.

4 As Figure 2.5 illustrates, you can make changes to those
commands and capabilities by selecting or deselecting the
desired options.

5 When you have finished, click **OK** and your changes will take
effect.

→ Summary

Customising a program like Microsoft Word really has a two-fold
purpose. First, setting up the program in a way that makes sense
to you, as the primary user, ultimately makes the application
easier for you to work. However, more than that, the easier a
program is, the more efficient you can become.

And while customising the appearance of Word, the capabilities of the Quick Access Toolbar and some of the advanced customisation features may take a little bit of time up front, these customisation settings will help you to save time further down the road.

In the next chapter, you'll learn how to start and open documents, add text and text elements to documents, and save and close those same documents. These are the skills you'll need as the basis for everything you'll be doing in Word.

3

Getting Started with Word Documents

Word documents can be used for a variety of tasks. For example, you can use a Word document to write a letter to a friend or your clients, you can create newsletters, fliers, websites and blog posts – the possibilities are endless.

In fact, it was once thought that Word should be used only for letters and the like. However, with newly enhanced graphic capabilities, Word can be used as a fairly robust desktop publishing application.

However, whether you're creating a simple memo or a multi-page newsletter, all Word documents are created, saved and closed equally.

→ Starting and Opening Word Documents

In order to work effectively with Word, you should have a certain comfort level with both creating Word documents and working with existing Word documents.

Although it's fairly simple to start the Word program to create a document, you don't want to have to close and re-open the program each time you need to create something new. Plus, that doesn't take into account the times when you need to open a Word document that you (or someone else) have already created.

Starting a New Document

The most basic function you'll use Word for is to create a document from scratch. That means, starting with a blank page. In Word, there are several ways to reach a blank page. The first

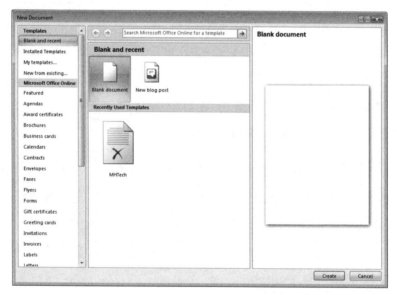

Figure 3.1
In the New Document dialogue box, Blank document has been selected by default.

way is to simply open the Word program. By default, Word always opens to a blank page when you launch the program.

But this approach isn't terribly effective if you already have the Word program open. Luckily, it's easy enough to create a brand new, blank document if the program is already open. Just follow these steps:

1 From any open document, click the **Office Menu** in the upper left corner of the page. The **Start** menu appears.

2 Select **New**. The **New Document** pane appears, as shown in Figure 3.1.

3 Click **Blank Page** (this option is selected by default) and click **OK.** A new blank document will open. The page you were previously working on will remain open until you close it.

Timesaver tip

To quickly create a new document based on the default Blank Page option, use the keyboard shortcut combination Ctrl+N.

Opening an Existing Document

Once you've created, saved and closed a document, you'll probably want to access that document again at another time. In Microsoft Word you can have several documents open at the same time. Depending upon your taskbar settings, each document occurrence is either represented by an individual button on the taskbar or you'll see a Word group that contains all open Word documents.

You can open an existing file in one of two ways: from within Microsoft Word and from the location where you have it stored.

To open a document from within Microsoft Word, follow these steps:

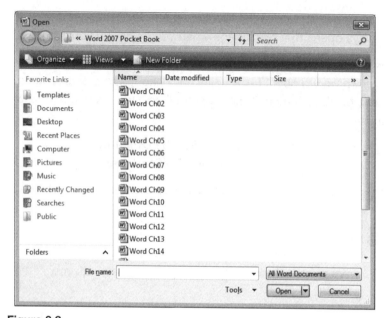

Figure 3.2
The Open dialogue box is where you can locate the file that you want to open.

1 Click the **Office Menu**.

2 Select **Open**. The Open dialogue box appears, as shown in Figure 3.2.

3 By default, the dialogue box will display the last location from which you opened a document. If you have never opened a document before, the default location is your My Documents folder. If your document is not in your My Documents folder, you can locate it from the Favourites link on the left side of the dialogue box.

4 When you have found the file you want to open, select it and click **Open**. The file is opened in Word.

Timesaver tip

To quickly access the **Open dialogue box**, use the keyboard shortcut combination Ctrl+O.

3

Timesaver tip

If you have recently worked with a document in Word, you can also open the file from the **Recent Documents** list. To access this list, click the **Office Menu**. The list appears on the right side of the menu. Just click the name of the file you want to open.

It is also possible to open a Word file even if you don't already have Word open. If that's how you want to access an existing file, follow these steps:

1 Click **Start.**

2 Navigate to the document that you want to open using the navigation bar on the right of the Start Menu.

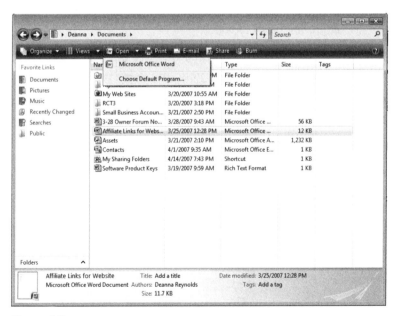

Figure 3.3
Select the Microsoft Office Word option to open the selected file with Word.

3 Select the document you want and click **Open.** A menu appears.

4 From the menu, select **Microsoft Office Word**, as shown in Figure 3.3.

Timesaver tip

Another way to open a file is to double-click on the file name. The file opens, just as if you had selected the file and then selected the **Open** command.

→ Adding Text to Your Documents

If you have a blank page sitting in front of you, you're going to want to add text to it. It's easy enough to do. Simply click inside the document and start typing.

The default font in Word is Calibri (Body), 11 point size. You can change this font from the **Font** group of the **Home** tab. Use the dropdown menu shown in Figure 3.4 to make your font selection.

Figure 3.4
You can change the font within a document from this menu.

The dropdown menu next to it is where you change the size of the font that you're using.

→ Saving and Closing Documents

When you've finished working with a document, you'll probably want to save the changes you've made to it before you close it. If you don't save the document, all of the changes will be lost and you may have to start all over again.

Follow these steps to save a document:

1 When you finish working in your document, click the **Office Menu.**

2 Hover the mouse over **Save As.** The **Save a copy of the document** menu appears.

3 From the menu, select the file format you would like to use, as shown in Figure 3.5.

- Word Document: Saves the document as a Word 2007 document (file extension .docx).

- Word Template: Saves the document as a Word 2007 Template (file extension .dotx).

- Word 97–2003 Document: Saves the document as a file that is compatible with Word 97–2003 (file extension .doc).

- Find add-ins for other file formats: This option allows you to download an **add-in** which enables Word documents to be saved as PDF or XPS formatted documents.

- Other formats: This opens a dialogue box that allows you to select additional formats to which you can save your document, as shown in Figure 3.6.

Figure 3.5
When you save your document the first time, you have several file formats from which to choose.

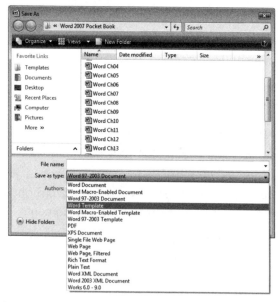

Figure 3.6
Additional file formats are available if the one you need isn't shown in the default listing.

4 Once you've chosen the file type that you want to save, the
Save As dialogue box appears. Select the location to which
you want the file saved from the **Favourites** link on the left
side of the page.

5 Enter the name you want the file to have in the **File Name**
box and click **Save.** The file will be saved in the location that
you specify.

Once you have named a document, saving it subsequently is
even easier. One way to save an existing document is to click the
Save icon in the Quick Access Toolbar. The icon looks like a
small floppy disk. You can also click the Office Menu button and
select **Save.**

Word does have an incremental backup saving method.
Periodically, it will save a temporary copy of your file in case the

program crashes. The file is stored in a temporary location and is accessible by the program only if there is a crash. If you close out of Word without saving, this temporary backup is automatically deleted. This means that if you lose a file during a crash, the temporary file might not include all of the information that was lost. It will restore only up to the last auto-save, which could have been several minutes in the past.

After you have saved your document, you can safely close it. Closing a document is easy – just click the red **X** in the top right corner of the page. Alternatively, you can select the Office Menu and then click **Close** from the menu that appears.

One thing that's different from previous versions of Word is that you can't close your document using the red **X** in the top right corner of the window and leave the Word window open. If you close out of the document using the red X, the whole Word window closes. If you need to access Word again, you'll have to use one of the methods listed in Chapter 1 for starting or opening a document. However, if you use the Office Menu to close the Word document, the Word window will remain open.

→ Summary

Starting and opening documents is as simple as clicking your mouse a few times. Entering text into a document is also pretty easy – it's really just click and type. Saving and closing the document requires only that you click a few buttons or commands and enter some naming information. But there's much more to Word 2007.

In the next chapter you'll learn about editing documents in Word. You'll get into more of the meat of the program and how to use it, including replacing and rearranging text, selecting and deleting text, and moving text between documents.

4

Editing Your Documents

The very moment you begin typing text into your Word documents is typically the very moment you're going to need to edit that same document. Microsoft Word knows that we're not perfect and offers us many ways to edit our documents after we've begun creating them.

Editing your documents means more than just replacing one word here or there. We're actually talking about moving efficiently around your document, highlighting text that you want to make changes to, permanently removing text, using the Clipboard, and moving text not only within the current document but also from one document to another.

→ Adding and Replacing Text

Adding text to an existing document is really no more difficult than simply clicking where you want the text to appear and then typing. As you type new text, the text located directly to the right of the blinking I-beam will automatically be pushed to the right, thus allowing you to effectively insert text without deleting existing text.

Important

Insert vs. Overtype Mode Typically, Microsoft Word operates in Insert mode. Essentially, this means when you add new text, the text to the right of your cursor simply pushes to the right to make room for the new text. However, you may occasionally wish to actually type over text already in your document. To do this, it's a good idea to delete the text you want to erase first, then add the new text. But if you want Word to consistently erase one character for every character you type, you need to enable Overtype mode. In previous versions of Word, you could switch between Insert and Overtype mode simply by pressing the Insert key on the keyboard. In Word 2007, this feature is disabled by default. However, you can enable this option by checking the box next to 'Use the Insert key to control overtype mode' in the Word Options dialogue box, as shown in Figure 4.1.

Replacing text, however, requires slightly more forethought, although it really isn't any more difficult than adding new text. To effectively replace text, you'll want to first either delete the text you're replacing or, at the very least, highlight the text you're replacing. Later in this chapter, we're going to look at the different ways you can select text. For now, just focus on highlighting text by dragging with your left mouse button.

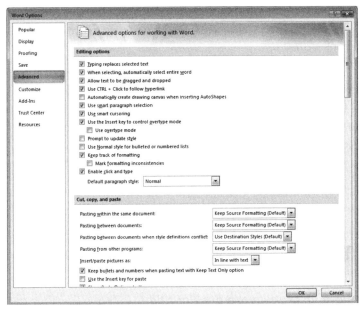

Figure 4.1
Use the Advanced section of the Options dialogue box to change how Word responds when you press the Insert key on the keyboard.

To replace text in your document, follow these steps:

1 Using the left mouse button, drag to **highlight the text** you want to replace.

2 **Type** the new text. The text that was highlighted will automatically be deleted the moment you begin typing the new text.

→ Navigating Your Document

Just as important as being able to efficiently edit the text in your documents is being able to efficiently navigate, or get around, the document. If you can master these techniques for moving around in a document, you will find that you'll often be able to complete your work in Word much quicker.

What's more, Word 2007 offers several ways to move around the document using both the keyboard and the mouse.

Navigating Using the Mouse

The quickest way to move between a document's pages is to use the mouse and the vertical scroll bar (located on the right side of the Word window). Keep in mind that when you move between pages using the mouse, you're not actually changing the position of the blinking I-beam.

To move up or down one **line** at a time, click the up arrow or the down arrow at either end of the vertical scroll bar.

To move up or down one **screen** at a time, click the blank area of the vertical scroll bar above the down arrow or below the up arrow.

To move up or down one **page** at a time, click the previous page and next page buttons located at the bottom of the vertical scroll bar.

Navigating Using the Keyboard

Although navigating between document pages is often faster using the mouse, you can move the cursor using even more methods with the keyboard.

Using the left, right, up and down arrow keys on the keyboard, you can move the blinking I-beam (or cursor location) **one character** or **one line** at a time. This is an efficient albeit slow way to move the cursor position.

To navigate a little bit faster, use these same arrow keys in conjunction with the Ctrl key on the keyboard. This way, you can move an entire **word** or **paragraph** each time you press one of the arrow keys.

To move quickly to the **beginning of any line** in which the I-beam is blinking, press the Home key on the keyboard. To move quickly to the **end of any line** in which the I-beam is blinking, press the End key on the keyboard.

Timesaver tip

To quickly move the cursor position to the top of the first page in the document, use the keyboard shortcut combination Ctrl+Home. Conversely, Ctrl+End moves the cursor to the bottom of the last page in the document.

You can also use the Page Up and Page Down keys to move the cursor **one screen** of information at a time. Or, combine Page Up and Page Down with the Ctrl keys to move the cursor one document **page** at a time.

→ Selecting Text

There are as many ways to select text as there are to navigate throughout your document, partly because many of the text selection techniques utilise the text navigation commands but also because Word often offers many ways to achieve the same result – something that will become more and more evident the longer you use Word. As you learn these new techniques, your job is not necessarily to remember all the ways you can perform a particular function in Word but to pick the way you find the easiest and stick with it.

Jargon buster

The terms **Select** and **Highlight** are often used interchangeably when referring to focusing Word on a specific range of text.

Knowing how to quickly select text may be more important than knowing how to navigate in a document. That's because selecting text is the key to being able to modify existing text.

Whether you want to apply bold formatting or move or copy the text, you can't do anything until you select the text you want to work with. As intuitive as Word can be with many functions, you still need to tell it what you want to change before you actually try to make the change. In Word, you do that by selecting text.

As with text navigation, you can use both mouse and keyboard techniques to select text. We're going to cover both.

Selecting Text Using the Mouse

To select one **word**, simply double-click the word.

To select one **line**, click once in the selection bar area of the document (this is the space directly to the left of the text that typically indicates the page margin).

To select one **paragraph**, either triple-click inside the paragraph or double-click in the selection bar area of the document.

To select the **entire document**, triple-click in the selection bar area of the document.

Selecting Text Using the Keyboard

When selecting text using the keyboard, the one key to remember is the Shift key.

To select text **one character** at a time, press and hold the Shift key while tapping the arrow keys (either right or left).

To select **one word** at a time, press and hold both the Shift and Ctrl keys while tapping the arrow keys (either right or left). Remember, holding Ctrl and pressing an arrow key moves the cursor one word at a time in the direction of the arrow key you have pressed. If you combine that with the Shift key, which extends any selection, you can select text one word at a time.

To select **one line** at a time, position the cursor at the beginning of the line, press and hold Shift, then press the End key. Once again, you're combining the text navigation technique of moving the cursor to the end of the line with the Shift key to extend a selection. This works in reverse as well. You can position the cursor at the end of the line, press and hold Shift and then press the Home key.

Timesaver tip

To quickly select the entire document, use the keyboard shortcut combination Ctrl+A.

Important

If the idea of using two hands to select text seems slightly overwhelming, you can jump into Selection (previously known as Extend) mode by pressing F8 on the keyboard. Once in Selection mode, you need to use the arrow keys on the keyboard only to move the cursor. As you move, text is automatically selected between the original cursor position and the direction the cursor is moving. Just remember to turn off Selection mode when you've finished (by pressing either Esc or F8). If you prefer to use the mouse, you can also right-click the Status Bar and choose Selection Mode from the shortcut menu to enable and disable Selection mode.

Selecting Text Using the Keyboard and the Mouse Together

If you don't mind using two hands, you can select some pretty cool areas of the document using the mouse and the keyboard together.

To select **one sentence**, press and hold the Ctrl key and click inside the sentence.

To select **one paragraph**, press and hold the Ctrl key and double-click inside the sentence.

Timesaver tip

Have you ever typed a document, such as an agenda, with times, dates or text on the left margin and related data lined up on a tab to the right? Then, after looking at the document decided the times (or information on the left) would look much better in bold? Instead of highlighting each individual time (or word), then formatting the text, you can use the non-contiguous selection technique to highlight a "column" of text in Word. To achieve this result, simply press and hold the Alt key while dragging with the left mouse button, beginning in the upper left corner of the text you want to select. Once the text is selected, you can format as usual.

→ Deleting Text

You've probably already figured out how to delete text. After all, there are very few of us lucky enough never to make a mistake. The easiest way to delete text that has already been entered on a Word document is to use either the Backspace or Delete keys on the keyboard.

However, when using Backspace or Delete, the process can become quite tedious if you have a lot of text to delete. After all, these keys remove text only one character at a time. That's fine for short words, but what if you need to delete an entire sentence, or worse, an entire paragraph?

In this case, select (or highlight) the text first, then press the Delete key on the keyboard. This way, you have to press the Delete key only once to delete an entire range of text.

Important

There's a small difference between using the Delete vs. Backspace keys and it's really all a matter of direction. Luckily the Backspace key on your keyboard typically has an arrow indicating the direction that the cursor moves. So, all you need to remember is that the Delete key works in the opposite direction. This means, each time you press the Backspace key one character at a time is deleted to the left of the blinking I-beam. Which means, each time you press the Delete key, one character at a time is deleted to the right of the blinking I-beam.

4

→ Copying, Cutting and Pasting Text

Word 2007 has made copying, cutting and pasting text easier than ever by placing these commands in the first group on the Home tab, as shown in Figure 4.2.

Figure 4.2
Use the Clipboard group on the Home tab to cut, copy and paste text.

Even better than the prominent placement of the cut, copy and paste commands in Word 2007 is that most Microsoft programs use the same techniques. This allows you to copy information contained in Word and paste into another Word document or a different Microsoft program altogether, such as an Excel spreadsheet or an Outlook e-mail message.

To copy text, follow these steps:

1 Select the text you want to copy.

2 Click the **Copy** button in the Clipboard group on the Home tab.

3 Position the cursor (blinking I-beam) in the document in which you want the copied text to appear.

4 Click the **Paste** button in the Clipboard group on the Home tab.

To move text, follow these steps:

1 Select the text you want to move.

2 Click the **Cut** button in the Clipboard group on the Home tab.

3 Position the cursor (blinking I-beam) in the document in which you want the cut text to appear.

4 Click the **Paste** button in the Clipboard group on the Home tab.

Jargon buster

When you **move** text, you are physically taking it from its original location and relocating it to an entirely new location in the current (or separate) document.

Jargon buster

When you **copy** text, the original text remains intact while you place another instance of the text in a new location in the current (or separate) document.

In addition to using the Ribbon to copy and move text, you can perform the same tasks by using a simple drag-and-drop method. To move or copy text using drag and drop, follow these steps:

1 Select the text you want to move (or copy).

2 Position the mouse on top of the highlighted text. When the mouse pointer changes to an arrow, press and hold the left mouse button.

3 **To move** the highlighted text, drag the blinking I-beam to the position in the document where you want the moved text to appear. Once the I-beam is in the new position, release the left mouse button. **To copy** the highlighted text, press and hold Ctrl and then drag the blinking I-beam to the position in the document where you want the moved text to appear. Once the I-beam is in the new position, release the left mouse button, then release the Ctrl key.

4

Timesaver tip

To quickly copy selected text to the Clipboard, use the keyboard shortcut combination Ctrl+C. You can just as easily use the keyboard shortcut combination Ctrl+X to cut text. When you're ready to paste cut or copied text, simply press Ctrl+V.

Using the Clipboard

Each time you click the Copy or Cut buttons on the Ribbon, the text is placed on the Windows Clipboard. This is what allows the information to be recalled later when the Paste button is clicked. Text that is added to the Windows Clipboard stays there until you cut or copy another set of text or you shut down your computer.

However, if you open the Clipboard task pane before you begin the cut or copy process, you can store up to 24 pieces of text to recall later. This means, you can actually copy up to 24 different bits of text, then paste them all into a new document or another area in the current document. The Clipboard task pane is shown in Figure 4.3.

In order for the Clipboard to be able to recall up to 24 bits of text, you need to open the Clipboard task pane first. You can open the Clipboard task pane using one of two methods.

Figure 4.3
Use the Clipboard task pane to keep track of up to 24 cut or copied bits of text.

Either:

- Cut or copy two bits of text without clicking the Paste button; or

- Click the Clipboard Dialogue Box Launcher arrow located in the lower right corner of the Clipboard group on the Home tab in the Ribbon.

Once the Clipboard Task Pane is open, simply select the text you want to move or copy and choose Cut or Copy as normal. Once you have the text on the Clipboard Task Pane, you'll need to determine whether you want to paste all of the information you've cut (or copied) or just individual pieces.

To paste everything contained on the Clipboard Task Pane, position the cursor in the document where you want the text to appear and then click the **Paste All** button at the top of the Clipboard Task Pane.

If, however, you want to paste only portions of text contained on the Clipboard Task Pane, position the cursor in the document where you want the text to appear, then click the bit of text on the Clipboard Task Pane you want to paste.

→ Moving Text Between Documents

Thanks to the Windows Clipboard, moving text between documents is easier than ever. If you understand how the cut, copy and paste functions work, using these functions between documents is nearly the same as using the cut, copy and paste functions within the same document.

This means, to move text between documents, you simply need to open the document that contains the original text. Then, select and cut or copy the text as normal. As you know, this puts the selected text on the Windows Clipboard – where it will stay until you shut down your computer (or cut or copy something else if the Clipboard Task Pane isn't open).

Next, open the document you want to paste the text into. This can be either a new or an existing document – either will work fine. Then, position the cursor where you want the cut or copied text to appear and click the Paste button in the Clipboard group on the Home tab in the Ribbon.

Timesaver tip

If you're looking for a quick way to move text between documents, before cutting or copying, open the document that contains the original text and the document you plan to paste the text into. Then, using the drag-and-drop move (or copy method), drag selected text from the original document to the button on the taskbar that represents the other document. That second document will open and you can continue using the drag-and-drop method. Just be sure you release the left mouse button only once you're sure the I-beam is blinking in the correct paste location.

→ Summary

Remember, being able to navigate quickly in your document can really boost your productivity. Just as important is your ability to accurately select the text that you want to work with – you'll see the importance of text selection over the next couple of chapters as we look at different formatting options in Word.

In the next chapter, you'll learn about adding visual appeal to your documents specifically through formatting with fonts, styles and text alignment.

5

Adding Visual Appeal to Your Documents

You'd be hard-pressed to find a person out there who doesn't appreciate visual appeal when added to a document. Many of the options for enhancing a document in Word are fairly intuitive. That's why you won't see a great deal of content in this book about applying formatting such as bold, italic and underline. Most people can find their way around Word well enough to know that all you need to do to apply this type of formatting is to click the appropriate button on the Home tab on the Ribbon.

Instead, we'll focus more on the results-oriented user interface that is brand new to Word 2007. One of the best ways to see this in action is in working with fonts. That's exactly where this chapter begins.

→ Working with Fonts

Any time you work with fonts, you're dealing with character formatting. And any time you work with character formatting, it's important to always highlight the text you're changing first, before you apply the formatting. Because character formatting can be applied to an individual character, it's typically necessary to select a character or set of characters that you are applying your formatting to, whether it's bold, italic, underline or any font face or font size change. Other types of character formatting include subscript, superscript, strikethrough and font colour.

However, when you work with paragraph formatting such as text alignment, selecting text isn't always necessary to achieve the desired result, as you'll see in the section "Working with Text Alignment".

Selecting Fonts

In Word 2007, the default font is Calibri, size 11. However, there are many more fonts to choose from in the Word 2007 program. All you need to do is click the dropdown arrow on the Font box in the Font group on the Home tab to see the wealth of fonts that you have access to, as shown in Figure 5.1.

With the new results-oriented user interface, choosing the font that best fits your document is much easier because now you can see a live preview of what a selected font might look like in your document before you make any permanent changes. To change the font, follow these steps:

1 Select the text you want to modify.

2 Click the Font dropdown arrow located in the Font group on the Home tab on the Ribbon.

3 As you hover your mouse over different font names, watch the live preview of the selected text in your document. When you find a font that suits the document, click the font name once with the left mouse button.

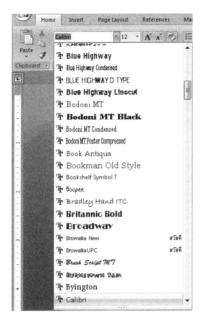

Figure 5.1
Click the Font dropdown arrow to see the myriad fonts available in Word 2007.

Timesaver tip

New to Word 2007 is the **Quick Format Mini Toolbar**. This is a shy little toolbar that pops up whenever you select text in the document. It's quite transparent at first, but if you move your mouse towards the **Quick Format Mini Toolbar**, it will gradually come into focus. Once it does, you'll notice it contains many of the most commonly used formatting commands, including font face, font size, bold, italic and text alignment.

Important

Of special note is the dialogue box launcher arrow located in the lower right corner of the Font group on the Home tab. Clicking this tiny arrow launches the Font dialogue box as shown in Figure 5.2 (a familiar face for those of us upgrading from previous versions of Word). In fact, you'll find these dialogue box Launcher arrows in the lower right corner of many of the new Ribbon groups. Hidden under these arrows are many of the old, familiar dialogue boxes from past versions of Word.

Figure 5.2
Clicking the dialogue box launcher arrow in the lower right corner of the Font group launches the Font dialogue box, giving you access to all the text character formatting options.

Setting the Default Font

Although the default font for all new Word 2007 documents is Calibri, size 11, that's certainly a setting that can be changed. To change the default font for all new documents, follow these steps:

1 Click the dialogue box launcher arrow located in the lower right corner of the Font group on the Home tab. This launches the Font Dialogue Box.

2 Select the desired default font attributes in the Font dialogue box.

3 Click the **Default** button, located in the lower left corner of the Font dialogue box. This launches the default font confirmation message, as shown in Figure 5.3.

4 Click **Yes**. This accepts the new font and returns you to the Font dialogue box.

5 Click **OK** to close the Font Dialogue Box.

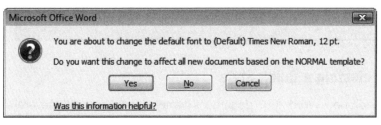

Figure 5.3
Before the default font for all new documents can be set, you need to verify that you want to make this global change.

Timesaver tip

To quickly open the **Font Dialogue Box**, use the keyboard shortcut combination Ctrl+D.

→ Working with Quick Styles

In a nutshell, Styles are saved sets of formatting. More than that, though, when used properly Styles can save you a great deal of formatting time in the long run. With Styles, you can apply a formatting consistency throughout your document that not only looks great but makes global document changes a cinch. If you find yourself changing the same headings or text in your document over and over, then you should probably give Styles a second look.

Some of these preset Styles hold a purpose beyond formatting your text. For instance, the Heading 1, Heading 2 and Heading 3

Styles can be used to generate a table of contents for your document. For more information on creating a table of contents, see Chapter 18.

> ### Jargon buster
>
> A **Quick Style** is a saved set of formatting that stores attributes such as fonts, colours and text alignment, among other visual effects.

Selecting a Quick Style

Each new Word 2007 document comes pre-loaded with several Quick Styles from which to choose, as you can see in Figure 5.4. You'll find Quick Styles located in the Styles group on the Home tab on the Ribbon.

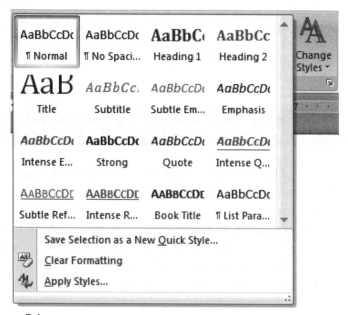

Figure 5.4
Each new Word 2007 document offers several Quick Styles, located in the Style Gallery.

Additionally, you can see the new live preview feature in action when you're selecting a Quick Style (similar to the live preview you see when changing the font). But since some Quick Styles rely on character formatting, be sure to select the text you're formatting before selecting a Quick Style. To apply a Quick Style to your document text, follow these steps:

1 Select the text you want to modify.

2 Click the **Quick Style Gallery** dropdown arrow located in the Styles group on the Home tab on the Ribbon.

3 As you hover your mouse over different quick styles, watch the live preview of the selected text in your document. Once you find a Quick Style that suits the document, click the Quick Style name once with the left mouse button.

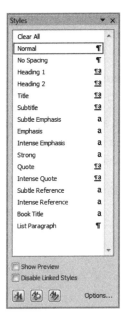

Figure 5.5
In lieu of using the Quick Styles Gallery, you can open the Quick Styles Task Pane by clicking the dialogue box launcher arrow located in the lower right corner of the Styles group.

Just as convenient is the Quick Styles Task Pane. If you find that a list of Quick Styles is easier to navigate, you can open the Quick Styles Task Pane for ready access to all of the Quick Styles, as shown in Figure 5.5. To open the Quick Styles Task Pane, click the dialogue box launcher arrow located in the lower right corner of the Styles group.

Creating and Saving Styles

Although Word 2007 offers several convenient Quick Styles, there are always times when you'll have your own unique set of formatting characteristics you'd like to save. To create a custom Quick Style, follow these steps:

1 Format the document text to include all of the formatting characteristics you'd like to save.

2 Click the dropdown arrow on the **Quick Style Gallery** located in the Styles group on the Home tab. The Quick Style Gallery opens.

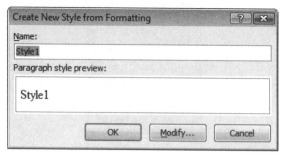

Figure 5.6
When creating a new quick style, you'll need to enter a name in the Create New Style from Formatting dialogue box.

3 Choose **Save Selection as New Quick Style** from the menu. The Create New Style from Formatting dialogue box opens as shown in Figure 5.6.

4 Enter a quick style name in the **Create New Style from Formatting** dialogue box.

5 Click **OK**. This confirms the new Quick Style and adds the Quick Style to the Quick Style Gallery for the active document.

Timesaver tip

Format Painter is one of the most under-used utilities in Microsoft Word. It's been around forever and it's a tremendous time-saver. Format Painter (located in the Clipboard group on the Home tab) was designed to copy formatting that's been applied to selected text. This allows you to then paste the copied formatting to other sets of selected text. Here's how it works. Just highlight text that has formatting applied which you want to copy and then click the Format Painter button once. Now select a second set of text and voilà! The formatting from the first set of selected text is copied to the second set. If you have multiple sets of text you want to copy the formatting to, just double-click the Format Painter button to keep it enabled – this allows you to paste the formatting to multiple sets of text. Just be sure to click the Format Painter button once when you've finished to turn the feature off.

Alternatively, you may choose to modify Word's built-in Quick Styles for an individual document. This way, you can still take advantage of advanced features (such as using the Heading 1, Heading 2 and Heading 3 Quick Styles to build a table of contents) and format your document to your preferred look – the best of both worlds! To modify one of Word's built-in Quick Styles, follow these steps:

1 Format the document text to include all of the formatting characteristics you'd like to save.

2 Select the newly formatted text.

3 Click the dropdown arrow on the **Quick Style Gallery** located in the Styles group on the Home tab. The Quick Style Gallery opens.

4 **Right-click** the Quick Style name that you'd like to update. The Quick Style shortcut menu appears, as shown in Figure 5.7.

5 Choose **Update [Style Name] to Match Selection** from the Quick Style shortcut menu. The Quick Style updates to match the formatting of the text you selected in Step 2 above.

Figure 5.7
When you right-click an existing Quick Style name in the Quick Styles Gallery, you can choose to update the Quick Style based on the text selection from the shortcut menu.

In contrast, you can also use the Apply Styles task pane to apply and modify Quick Styles in your document. To open the Apply Styles task pane, follow these steps:

1 Click the dropdown arrow on the **Quick Style Gallery** located in the Styles group on the Home tag. The Quick Style Gallery opens.

2 Choose **Apply Styles**, located at the bottom of the Quick Styles Gallery. The Apply Styles task pane opens, as shown in Figure 5.8.

- To apply a Quick Style to document text using the Apply Styles task pane, select the document text, then select the quick style name in the Apply Styles task pane.

- To modify a Quick Style using the Apply Styles task pane, select the Quick Style name to modify, then click **Modify** in the Apply Styles task pane. Make your changes, then click **OK**.

Figure 5.8
The Apply Styles task pane can also be opened using the keyboard
shortcut combination Ctrl+SHIFT+S.

Timesaver tip

You can open the **Apply Styles task pane** by using the keyboard
shortcut combination Ctrl+Shift+S.

→ Working with Text Alignment

Text alignment refers to the horizontal position of text on a
document page. There are basically only a few options when
working with text alignment:

- **Left Align** – lines up all text in a paragraph along the left
  indent.

- **Centre Align** – centres all text in a paragraph between the left
  and right indents.

- **Right Align** – lines up all text in a paragraph along the right
  indent.

- **Justify** – spaces all text in a paragraph equally so as to align
  text along both the left and right indents.

Many people assume (incorrectly) that text is aligned between the page margins. Although it may appear that way on the surface, text is actually aligned between the left and right indents. Since the default position for the left and right indents is zero inches from the left and right margins, you can see why people tend to come to this conclusion.

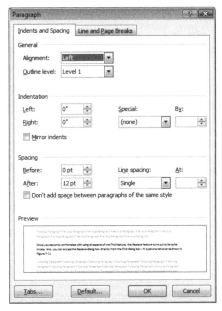

Figure 5.9
Clicking the dialogue box launcher arrow in the lower right corner of the Paragraph group launches the Paragraph dialogue box, giving you access to all of the paragraph formatting options, including alignment.

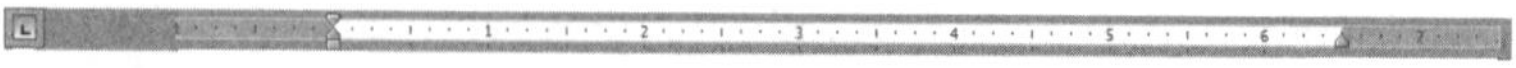

Figure 5.10
Left and right indents are indicated on the ruler bar as triangles located on the left and right margins.

Although indents can be set using the Paragraph dialogue box, it's often easier to work with indents using the ruler bar. We'll cover indents more in depth in Chapter 8. For now, just take note of the triangles located on the ruler bar (located at 0″ and 6½″), shown in Figure 5.10. Those are the Indent markers. You can see how they line up exactly with the margins.

Since text alignment is paragraph formatting, it isn't necessary to select text prior to assigning your chosen alignment (unless you want to change the alignment for multiple paragraphs). To change text alignment, follow these steps:

1 Position the cursor inside the paragraph you want to modify (or select multiple paragraphs).

2 Click the appropriate alignment option (left, centre, right or justify).

Timesaver tip

There are a few handy keyboard combination shortcuts to use when working with text alignment. What's nice about the following shortcuts is that they work in many Windows-based programs, including Word.

To:	Press:
Left align	Ctrl+L
Centre align	Ctrl+E
Right align	Ctrl+R
Justify	Ctrl+J

5

→ Summary

Adding visual appeal to your documents may make the difference between a document that's read versus one that's simply tossed aside. Using the techniques in this chapter, hopefully your documents will fall into the "read" category.

In the next chapter, we'll continue with the "visual appeal' theme as we learn about adding borders and font colour. For added impact, we'll also cover working with backgrounds, watermarks and cover pages.

6

Adding Borders and Colour

It's always amazing how a small splash of colour and creativity can really spice up your document. Colour can turn once lifeless streams of plain text into something that draws in a reader's attention and, more importantly, keeps them interested.

In this chapter, we'll move beyond font colour as we explore adding borders and entire page background colours, among other topics. In Word 2007, there's also a terrific new feature for quickly adding preformatted cover pages.

→ Adding and Changing Borders

When you're looking to add a certain level of visual interest to your document, borders definitely fit the bill. The nice thing about borders is that they can be added to individual paragraphs as well as to an entire page. Word 2007 comes with several borders you can use and customise.

Let's start with adding borders to selected paragraphs. Like text alignment, borders follow indents. This means, adding a border around a paragraph creates a box around the entire paragraph that lines up on the left with the left indent and on the right with the right indent. The top and bottom lines of the box are determined by any spacing that's been added either above or below the paragraph, respectively. (For more information on line and paragraph spacing, see Chapter 8.) To add a border to a paragraph, follow these steps:

Figure 6.1
The Borders dropdown menu located in the Paragraph group on the Home tab offers many border options for your paragraphs.

1 Click inside the paragraph to which you want to apply the border (or select multiple paragraphs).

2 Click the **Borders** dropdown arrow located in the Paragraph group on the Home tab. This opens the Borders menu, as shown in Figure 6.1.

3 Click the border style you want to apply. This applies a border to the selected paragraph(s).

Important

To remove any border once it's been added, click inside the paragraph with the border, click the dropdown arrow next to the Borders command and choose No Border from the dropdown menu.

For more control over how the borders appear and their thickness, you can open the Borders and Shading dialogue box, shown in Figure 6.2. To open the Borders and Shading dialogue box, follow these steps:

1 Click inside the paragraph to which you want to apply the border (or select multiple paragraphs).

2 Click the **Borders** dropdown arrow located in the Paragraph group on the Home tab. This opens the Borders menu, as shown in Figure 6.1.

3 Click the **Borders and Shading** link at the bottom of the menu. This opens the Borders and Shading dialogue box, shown in Figure 6.2.

4 Once the Borders and Shading dialogue box is open, you have several options, including:

- **Setting**: Under Setting, you can choose a predefined border format such as Box, Shadow or 3-D.

- **Style**: Under Style, you can choose the type of border you want to apply. For instance, you can opt for a dotted, dashed or solid line.

- ■ **Color**: Under Color, you can choose the colour of the border you want to apply.

- ■ **Width**: Under Width, you can choose the weight of the border line. In other words, width refers to the thickness of the line.

The beauty in using the Borders and Shading dialogue box is the level of control you're given in applying a border to a paragraph. With this box, you can pick a different line style, colour and width for each border. This means, your border could feasibly display with a dotted blue line along the top, a dashed black line along the bottom and solid yellow lines on either side.

To achieve this type of effect, for each line style you want to apply, set your style colour and width preferences, then click the corresponding line on the right side of the dialogue box under Preview. Repeat for each line style.

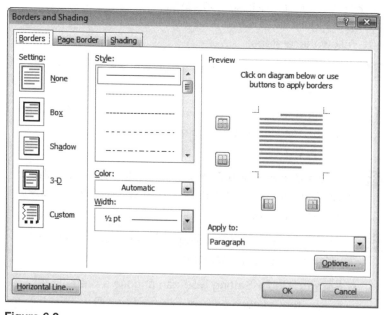

Figure 6.2
Selecting Borders and Shading from the Borders menu located in the Paragraph group on the Home tab opens the Borders and Shading dialogue box.

In addition to paragraph borders, you can create page borders that surround your entire page. Although adding page borders is a process very similar to adding paragraph borders, there is one additional option – border art. To add a page border, follow these steps:

1 Click inside the page to which you want to apply the page border.

2 Click the **Borders** dropdown arrow located in the Paragraph group on the Home tab. This opens the Borders and Shading menu, as shown in Figure 6.1.

3 Click the **Borders and Shading** link at the bottom of the menu. This opens the Borders and Shading dialogue box, shown in Figure 6.2.

4 Click the **Page Border** tab. This opens the Page Border options in the Borders and Shading dialogue box, as shown in Figure 6.3.

5 Once on the Page Border tab, many of the options are identical to applying a paragraph border. However, there is one additional option:

- **Art**: Under Art, you can choose a predefined border art format such as apples, birthday cakes, stars and many more.

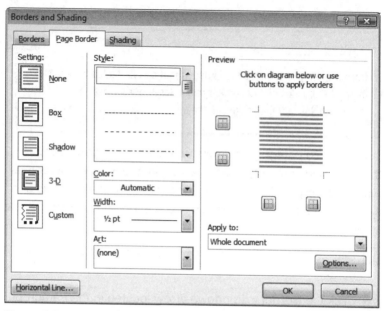

Figure 6.3
The Page Border tab in the Borders and Shading dialogue box offers a wealth of options for creating a custom border that surrounds each individual page in your document.

→ Changing Font Colours

Here we go again with character versus paragraph formatting. You'll recall from the last chapter that certain types of formatting can be applied to one character at a time – font colour is one of those types. This means that text selection is necessary in order to properly apply font colour formatting to any text. However, since you already know how to apply other types of character formatting such as fonts, applying font colours should seem fairly intuitive. To apply font colour formatting, follow these steps:

1 Select the text you want to modify.

2 Click the dropdown arrow next to the font colour command in the Font group on the Home tab. This displays the available font colour choices, as shown in Figure 6.4.

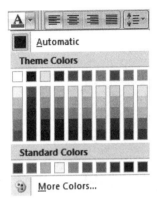

Figure 6.4
Several font colours are available and can be seen by clicking the dropdown arrow next to the Font Color command located in the Font group on the Home tab.

3 Hover your mouse over the different font colours noticing live preview in action on the document. Click the font colour of your choice.

Timesaver tip

Font Color is one of the commands located on the **Quick Format Mini Toolbar**. The next time you are looking to modify text font colour, select the text, then look for the Quick Format Mini Toolbar.

For more advanced colour options, click the More Colors link located at the bottom of the Font dropdown menu. Clicking this link opens the Colors dialogue box, as shown in Figure 6.5. This dialogue box offers two tabs full of colour choices.

The Standard tab (shown in Figure 6.5) offers a wide range of standard colours. To apply one of these colours to selected text, simply click the chosen colour, then click the OK button.

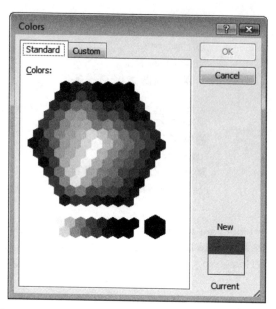

Figure 6.5
Known simply as the colour "beehive", you have access to a wealth of colour options in the Colors dialogue box.

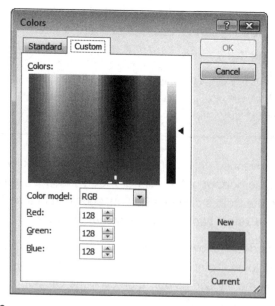

Figure 6.6
The Custom tab in the Colors dialogue box offers a greater range of colour choices for your text.

For more advanced colour options, click the Custom tab in the Colors dialogue box shown in Figure 6.6. Using the Custom tab, drag the colour marker in the centre of the colour swatch to a colour range. Then, using the slider on the right side of the colour range, choose the colour brightness level. You'll see a comparison in the lower right corner of the current colour (on the bottom) versus the new colour (on the top). Once your chosen colour is shown in the new colour area of this dialogue box, simply click OK to apply the chosen colour to your selected text.

Timesaver tip

New to Word 2007 are **Themes**. Themes allow you to quickly apply uniform formatting to an entire document. Each theme contains a set of design elements that stores colours, fonts and graphics. Themes are located on the Page Layout tab on the Ribbon. In the Themes group, there is a command specifically for document colours. Using this command applies a predefined colour scheme to your entire document. For more information on Themes, see Chapter 9.

→ Changing Background Colours

When it comes to background colours, there are a couple of different options worth mentioning. You can apply colour to individual paragraphs, known as shading. Or you can apply colour to an entire page, known as a background.

Applying colour to an individual paragraph means playing by the same rules as applying borders. Essentially, paragraph colours (shading) follow the paragraph indents on the left and right and the paragraph before and after spacing on the top and bottom. To add shading to a paragraph, follow these steps:

1 Click inside the paragraph to which you want to apply the shading (or select multiple paragraphs).

2 Click the **Shading** dropdown arrow located in the Paragraph group on the Home tab. This opens the Shading menu, as shown in Figure 6.7.

3 Hover the mouse over possible shading options. You'll notice live preview in effect as the selected paragraph(s) changes to match the possible shading choices. Click the shading colour you want to apply. This applies shading to the selected paragraph(s).

Important

The Shading dropdown menu has a More Colors option similar to the Borders and Shading dropdown menu. It's important to point out that these two options work identically. Clicking the More Colors option in the Shading dropdown menu opens the same Colors dialogue box as the More Colors option found on the Borders dropdown menu.

In addition to paragraph shading, you can create page backgrounds that encompass your entire document. Although page backgrounds may seem similar to paragraph backgrounds (shading) on the surface, there is one major difference. Page backgrounds don't print, but paragraph backgrounds do. To add a page background, follow these steps:

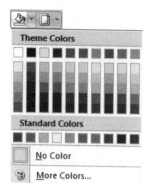

Figure 6.7
The Shading dropdown menu located in the Paragraph group on the Home tab offers many shading options for your paragraphs.

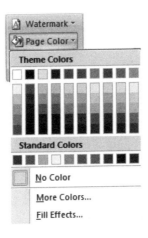

Figure 6.8
The Page Color dropdown menu located in the Page Background group on the Page Layout tab offers many colour options for your document pages.

1 Click the **Page Color** command in the Page Background group on the Page Layout tab on the Ribbon. The Page Color dropdown menu opens, as shown in Figure 6.8.

2 Hover the mouse over possible page colour options. You'll notice live preview in effect as the active page changes to match the possible colour choices. Click the colour you want to apply. This applies colour to the document.

Important

To remove a page background once a colour has been applied, simply click the Page Color command and choose No Color from the dropdown menu.

Beyond simple colours, in fact even beyond the custom colours found in the Color dialogue box, page backgrounds offer even more options when you choose the Fill Effects option from the Page Color dropdown menu shown in Figure 6.8. Clicking Fill Effects from this menu opens the Fill Effects dialogue box with four additional page background options:

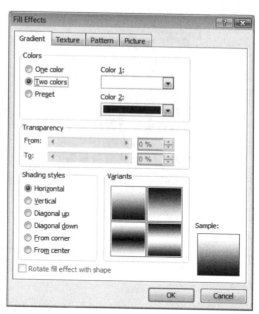

Figure 6.9
Using the Gradient option, you can apply a gradual progression of one or two colours (of your choice) that flows from one colour to the next.

- **Gradient**: Using the Gradient option, you can apply a gradual progression of one or two colours (of your choice) that flows from one colour to the next. Or you can choose a gradual progression from one shade to the next based on one single colour. The Gradient tab of the Fill Effects dialogue box is shown in Figure 6.9.

- **Texture**: Using the Texture option, you can apply common texture patterns such as a basket weave or marbled appearance to your page background. The Texture tab of the Fill Effects dialogue box is shown in Figure 6.10.

- **Pattern**: Using the Pattern option, you can apply both a foreground and a background colour with a series of lines or dots that forms a pattern. Patterns are extremely versatile when trying to display differences on a black and white printer. The Pattern tab of the Fill Effects dialogue box is shown in Figure 6.11.

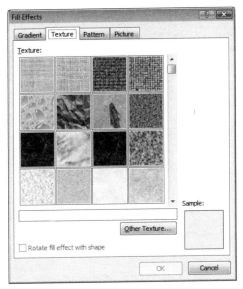

Figure 6.10
Using the Texture option, you can apply common texture patterns
such as a basket weave or marbled appearance to your page
background.

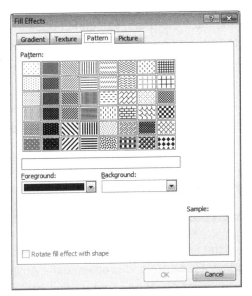

Figure 6.11
Using the Pattern tab, you can apply both a foreground and a
background colour with a series of lines or dots that forms a pattern.

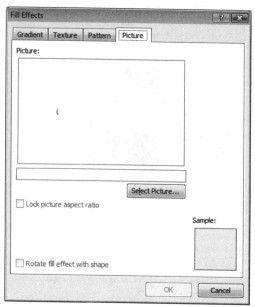

Figure 6.12
Using the Picture tab, you can choose to display an image located on your computer as the page background.

- **Picture**: Using the Picture tab, you can choose to display an image located on your computer as the page background. The Picture tab of the Fill Effects dialogue box is shown in Figure 6.12.

As you can see, there are many options for adding backgrounds to your pages, whether to individual paragraphs or to entire documents.

→ Adding Cover Pages

A cover page is the first page in a document that indicates the document's contents, author and creation date. Acting as a welcoming page, cover pages can add a great deal of flow to a document. In Word 2007, the guesswork has been taken out of creating cover pages. To insert a cover page, follow these steps:

1 Click the **Cover Page** command in the Pages group on the Insert tab. The Cover Page Gallery displays, as shown in Figure 6.13.

2 Select a cover page. The cover page is added to your document as the first page.

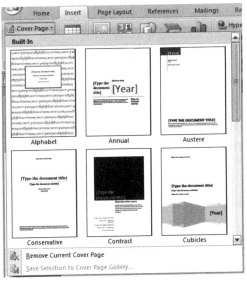

Figure 6.13
There are several cover page choices found in the Cover Page Gallery located in the Pages group on the Insert tab.

Jargon buster

A **cover page** is the first page in a document that indicates the document's contents, author and creation date.

Timesaver tip

To remove a cover page that's been added using the Cover Page Gallery, simply click the Cover Page command and choose Remove Current Cover Page.

→ Adding Watermarks

A watermark consists of text or pictures that appear behind your document text on every page, often in a faded colour. For instance, a watermark often looks like a stamp and includes text such as "Confidential" or "Draft". Some companies choose to use their company logo as a watermark.

Jargon buster

A **watermark** consists of text or pictures that appear behind your document text on every page, often in a faded colour. Common watermarks include the text "Confidential" or "Draft". Some companies use their company logo as a watermark.

Word 2007 comes with four predefined watermarks:

- Confidential (horizontal)
- Confidential (diagonal)
- Draft (horizontal)
- Draft (diagonal)

To add a predefined watermark to a document, follow these steps:

1 Click the **Watermark** command located in the Page Background group on the Page Layout tab. This opens the Watermark dropdown menu, shown in Figure 6.14.

2 Click the predefined watermark of your choice.

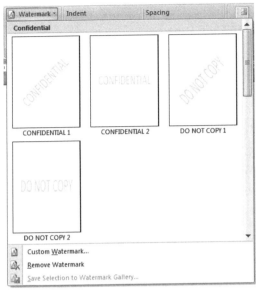

Figure 6.14
There are four predefined watermarks found in the Watermark Gallery located in the Page Background group on the Page Layout tab.

Important

When viewing your document, you can see watermarks only in Print Layout View, Full Screen Reading View and Print Preview. And, of course, you'll see the watermark on the printed document. This means when viewing the document in Outline, Draft or Web Layout View, watermarks are not visible.

In addition to the predefined watermarks, you can create your own text-based watermarks or use graphics stored on your computer as a watermark. To create a custom watermark, follow these steps:

1 Click the **Watermark** command located in the Page Background group on the Page Layout tab. This opens the Watermark dropdown menu, shown in Figure 6.14.

2 Click **Custom Watermark** from the Watermark

dropdown menu. The Watermark dialogue box opens, as shown in Figure 6.15.

- **To create a custom picture watermark**: Click the option button next to Picture Watermark, then click Browse to locate an image stored on your computer. You can also set the scale (or, size) of the graphic and choose whether or not the image should appear with a washout effect.

- **To create a custom text watermark**: Click the option button next to Text Watermark, then either select text in the Text box or type your own text-based watermark. You can also set the font, font size, colour and layout of the custom text watermark.

3 When you have finished setting custom options for either the text or the picture watermark, click **OK** to apply the watermark to the current document.

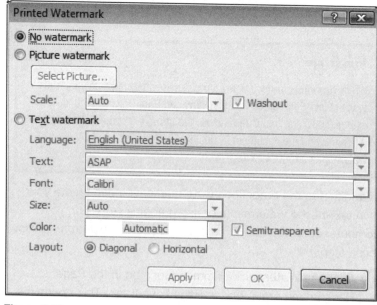

Figure 6.15
Clicking Custom Watermark in the Watermark dropdown menu displays options for creating custom text and picture watermarks.

→ Summary

Simply stated, adding visual impact with borders and colours will give your documents a "wow" effect. And who among us couldn't use a "wow" effect now and then? After all, adding elements such as cover pages, backgrounds and watermarks has been so streamlined; you'll be hard-pressed to find a reason *not* to use them.

In the next chapter, we'll cover some very important proofreading tools. Spell Check is such a simple feature to use that it can be perplexing to see documents with typos in them these days. More than that, however, we'll get into features such as Word Count and Thesaurus as well as other Word 2007 proofreading options.

6

7

Using Proofreading Tools

It seems every version of Microsoft Word is more intuitive and flexible than its predecessor. That's good news because it means you have to spend less time proofreading. Some proofing tools such as Spell Check, Grammar Check and AutoCorrect are always working in the background as you type. Other proofing tools that are available upon request include Find and Replace, Thesaurus and Research Services.

→ Spell Check and AutoCorrect

After spending time creating the perfect document, the last thing you want to do is proof it. But without proofing you risk sending out a document full of errors. Luckily, Word 2007 has a few quick and easy features that help you knock out the proofing work so you can get back to work.

Jargon buster

Spell Check is a feature that scans your Word document for spelling errors and provides suggestions for misspelled words.

Word's Spell Check feature, when started, scans your document from top to bottom, offering suggestions for each misspelled word (or grammar etiquette violation). To run Spell Check, follow these steps:

1 Click the **Spelling and Grammar** command located in the Proofing group on the Review tab on the Ribbon. The Spelling and Grammar dialogue box opens, as shown in Figure 7.1.

2 For each spelling (or grammar) error, choose from the following options:

- **Ignore Once** – ignores this occurrence of the misspelled word.

- **Ignore All** – ignores all occurrences of the misspelled word.

- **Add to Dictionary** – adds the word, as spelled in the document, to the custom dictionary (Custom.dic).

- **Change** – changes the misspelled word for the selected suggestion.

- **Change All** – changes all occurrences of the misspelled word for the selected suggestion.

- **AutoCorrect** – corrects the misspelled word to the matching AutoCorrect entry.

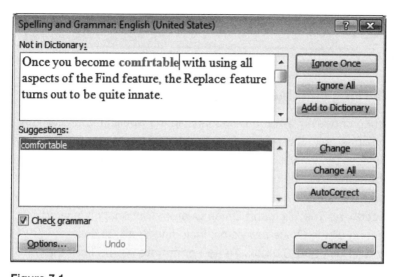

Figure 7.1
The Spell Check feature scans your document from top to bottom, offering suggestions for each misspelled word or grammar etiquette violation.

3 Once you choose one of the options in the Spelling and Grammar dialogue box, Word automatically moves to the next error in the document. When the Spell Check is complete, click **OK** when prompted, as shown in Figure 7.2.

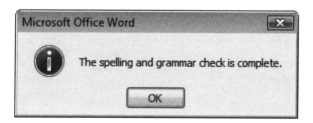

Figure 7.2
After completing the Spell Check process, you are rewarded with a successful completion message.

Working with the Custom Dictionary

When choosing "Add to Dictionary" in the Spelling and Grammar dialogue box, chosen words are added to the Microsoft Office Custom Dictionary. The Custom Dictionary is a list of words added by you, the user, which typically consists of pronouns and industry-specific terms that wouldn't be found in a general dictionary. The Microsoft Office Custom Dictionary is shared among all the Office programs, including Word, Excel, PowerPoint and Outlook. To add or remove words from the Custom Dictionary, follow these steps:

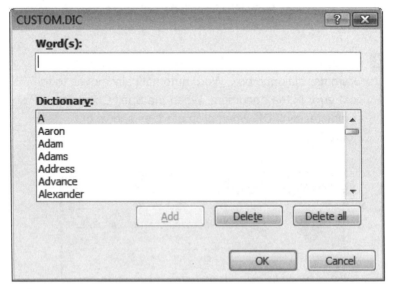

Figure 7.3
The Custom Dictionary is shared among all Office programs and contains a list of words added by you, the user.

1 Open the Office Menu and choose **Word Options**. This opens the Word Options dialogue box.

2 Click **Proofing**. This displays the Word options related to proofing tasks.

3 Click **Custom Dictionaries**. This opens the list of dictionaries available to Word for use during proofing tasks, such as Spell Check.

4 Click **Edit Word List**. This open the Custom Dictionary word list, as shown in Figure 7.3.

5 Add or remove words as necessary. Click **OK** to close the Custom Dictionary word list.

6 Click **OK** to close the dictionary list.

7 Click **OK** to close the Word Options dialogue box.

Timesaver tip

You may find yourself "Ignoring" the same misspelled word over and over again. Each time you run Spell Check, Word tends to pick up the same words. To avoid this, consider adding a word that Word thinks is a typo to the Custom Dictionary. To do this, when running Spell Check, click Add to Dictionary any time Word highlights a word it doesn't recognise.

Just like Spell Check, AutoCorrect can be a real time-saver. AutoCorrect automatically works behind the scenes correcting commonly misspelled words as you type. In fact, AutoCorrect is so fast, you may not even realise every time it corrects a typo. To test this theory, open a new document and type "teh". You should notice two things happening:

■ The letters "teh" are immediately corrected to "the".

■ The word becomes capitalised as "The".

Both of these corrections are instinctive functions of AutoCorrect. What's more, AutoCorrect is enabled, by default. This means you don't have to do anything (expect misspell words) to get AutoCorrect to function.

Jargon buster

AutoCorrect automatically works behind the scenes correcting commonly misspelled words as you type. In fact, AutoCorrect is so fast, you may not even realise every time it corrects a typo.

To see which words AutoCorrect fixes, follow these steps:

1 Click the **Office Button**. This opens the Office Menu.

2 Click **Word Options**. This opens the Word Options dialogue box.

3 Click **Proofing**. This displays the Word options related to proofing tasks.

4 Click **AutoCorrect Options**. This opens the AutoCorrect Options dialogue box, as shown in Figure 7.4.

Timesaver tip

When you need to insert a common symbol such as © (copyright), ® (registered) or ™ (trademark), use the AutoCorrect feature. Each of these symbols already resides in the AutoCorrect list. To insert these symbols use:
(c) to insert the copyright symbol "©"
(r) to insert the registered symbol "®"
(tm) to insert the trademark symbol "™"

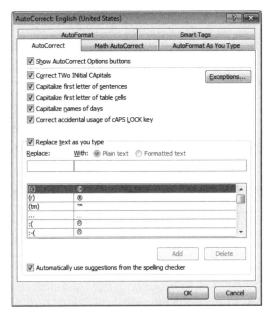

Figure 7.4
To see which words are corrected instinctively by the AutoCorrect feature, open the AutoCorrect Options dialogue box.

Customising the AutoCorrect List

You can customise the AutoCorrect list to better suit your needs. For instance, you may need to remove the AutoCorrect entry that changes "HTE" to "THE" because you use the acronym "HTE" in your documents.

To add or remove an AutoCorrect entry, follow these steps:

1 Click the **Office Button**. This opens the Office Menu.

2 Click **Word Options**. This opens the Word Options dialogue box.

3 Click **Proofing**. This displays the Word options related to proofing tasks.

4 Click **AutoCorrect Options**. This opens the AutoCorrect Options dialogue box, as shown in Figure 7.4.

5 Either:

- Locate and select the AutoCorrect entry you want to remove. Click **Delete**. This deletes the selected AutoCorrect entry.

- Type the acronym you want to replace in the Replace: box. Type the word you want AutoCorrect to insert in place of the acronym in the With: box. Click **Add**. This adds the entry to the AutoCorrect list.

6 Click **OK**. This closes the AutoCorrect Options dialogue box.

7 Click **OK**. This closes the Word Options dialogue box.

Timesaver tip

If the AutoCorrect feature corrects a word unnecessarily, you can either remove the entry from the AutoCorrect list or simply press the Undo button.

Timesaver tip

If you find yourself typing the same phrases often, consider adding those phrases as AutoCorrect options. In fact, you can even add formatted text to the AutoCorrect list. To add multiple lines or formatted text as an AutoCorrect entry, type the full entry in a Word document, then select the text. With the text selected, open the AutoCorrect Options dialogue box. You'll see the highlighted text in the With: portion of this box. Now all you need to add is the acronym, clicking Add when you've finished.

→ Proofing as You Type

After spending just a few minutes in Word, you will probably have seen "Proofing as you type" in action. Any time you misspell a word, Word underlines the word with a red, wavy line – that is, when AutoCorrect doesn't automatically fix the misspelled word for you.

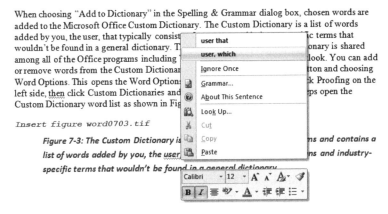

When choosing "Add to Dictionary" in the Spelling & Grammar dialog box, chosen words are added to the Microsoft Office Custom Dictionary. The Custom Dictionary is a list of words added by you, the user, that typically consist [...] ic terms that wouldn't be found in a general dictionary. T[...] onary is shared among all of the Office programs including [...] look. You can add or remove words from the Custom Dictiona[...] tton and choosing Word Options. This opens the Word Option[...] k Proofing on the left side, then click Custom Dictionaries and [...] ps open the Custom Dictionary word list as shown in Fig[...]

`Insert figure word0703.tif`

Figure 7-3: The Custom Dictionary is [...] ns and contains a list of words added by you, the user [...] ns and industry-specific terms that wouldn't be found in a general dictionary.

Figure 7.5
Using "Proofing As You Type" allows you to correct misspelled words on the spot without having to run the Spell Check feature.

Using the "Proofing as you type" feature allows you to spot spell check your document as you're typing. Whenever you see a word with a red, wavy underline, right-click the word. When you do, a shortcut menu appears, as shown in Figure 7.5. At the top of the shortcut menu is a list of possible word corrections. Simply click the correctly spelled word and continue typing.

→ Using Grammar Check

Just as the "Proofing as you type" feature adds a red, wavy line under any misspelled words, the grammar check feature adds the green, wavy line under any phrase or sentence that doesn't meet proper grammar etiquette. Common errors that Grammar Check can pick up include:

- Subject–verb agreement

- Incomplete and run-on sentences

- Noun phrases

- Possessive and plurals

- Punctuation

You can correct grammar errors the same way you correct "Proofing as you type" errors – simply right-click the sentence that contains the grammar error and choose the correction from the shortcut menu.

Jargon buster

The **Grammar Check** feature checks your document's sentences to ensure they conform to standard grammar etiquette. Grammar Check scans your document looking for common grammar errors – too many to list here. However, the most common grammar errors include fragments and run-on sentences as well as improper punctuation around quotation marks.

Although Grammar Check follows the most common grammar etiquette guidelines, you can customise the errors the Grammar Check feature flags. To customise Grammar Check, follow these steps:

1 Click the **Office Button**. This opens the Office Menu.

2 Click **Word Options**. This opens the Word Options dialogue box.

3 Click **Proofing**. This displays the Word options related to proofing tasks.

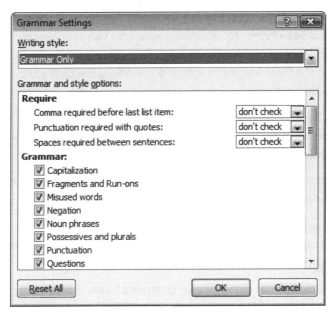

Figure 7.6
Although Grammar Check follows the most common grammar etiquette guidelines, you can customise the errors the Grammar Check feature flags.

4 Click **Settings** (next to Writing Style). This opens the Grammar Settings dialogue box, as shown in Figure 7.6.

5 Set your Grammar Settings preferences.

6 Click **OK** to close the Grammar Settings dialogue box.

7 Click **OK** to close the Word Options dialogue box.

→ Using Find and Replace

If you need to locate specific text in your Word document, you can save a tremendous amount of time by getting Word to search the document for you using the Find feature. Chances are good that if you rely on your eyesight to locate all occurrences of a specific word or phrase, you'll miss at least one. But if you get Word to search the document for you, you can rest assured that all occurrences of your chosen word or phrase will be located. To use the Find feature to locate a specific word or phrase, follow these steps:

1 Click the **Find** command found in the Editing group on the Home tab on the Ribbon. The Find dialogue box opens, as shown in Figure 7.7.

2 Type the word or phrase for which you're searching in the **Find what** box.

3 Click **Find next**. Word locates and highlights the next occurrence of your word or phrase in the document. Click **Find next** again to locate the next occurrence.

4 Click **Cancel** when you've completed searching the document.

Timesaver tip

To highlight all occurrences of your selected word or phrase, instead of clicking Find next in the Find dialogue box, click Reading Highlight, then Highlight All. This technique highlights all occurrences of your selected word or phrase in the document.

Figure 7.7
Click the Find command found in the Editing group on the Home tab on the Ribbon to open the Find dialogue box.

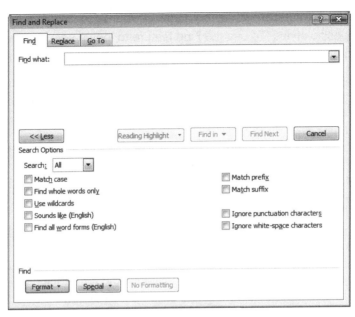

Figure 7.8
With this expanded Find and Replace dialogue box, you can further define your search criteria to search for whole words only or words that match a specific case.

For a more advanced search, click the **More** button in the Find dialogue box. When you click the More button, the Find and Replace dialogue box expands, as shown in Figure 7.8. With this expanded box, you can further define your search criteria to search for whole words only or words that match a specific case.

For instance, when searching for the word "cat", the Find feature will locate all occurrences of the letters C-A-T in the document, whether those letters occur at the beginning, end or middle of another word. But clicking the "Find whole words only" check box will limit the search results to only the word "cat".

You can further define your search criteria by searching for words that match specific formatting. To define this formatting, after clicking the More button to expand the Find and Replace dialogue box, click the Format button found in the lower left corner. This gives you access to search for text that contains specific formatting such as bold text, double-spaced paragraphs or specific styles. To use the Find feature to locate specifically formatted text, follow these steps:

1 Click the **Find** command found in the Editing group on the Home tab on the Ribbon. The Find dialogue box opens, as shown in Figure 7.7.

2 Click the **More** button. The Find and Replace dialogue box expands, as shown in Figure 7.8.

3 Type the word or phrase for which you're searching in the **Find what** box.

4 Click the **Format** button. The Format menu opens, as shown in Figure 7.9.

5 Choose the option that best describes the formatting for which you are searching (i.e. click Font to search for bold

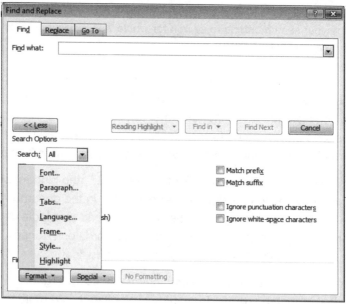

Figure 7.9
The Format menu gives you access to search for text that contains specific formatting such as bold text, double-spaced paragraphs or specific styles.

formatting, Styles to search for a specific style, or Paragraph to search for paragraph formatting such as double-spacing).

6 Click **Find next**. Word locates and highlights the next occurrence of your word or phrase in the document. Click **Find next** again to locate the next occurrence.

7 Click **Cancel** when you've completed searching the document.

In addition to searching for plain text and text that contains formatting, you can search for specific non-printing characters such as hard returns, line breaks and tabs. Each of these non-printing characters and more can be found by clicking the Special button at the bottom of the Find and Replace dialogue box. To use the Find feature to locate non-printing characters, follow these steps:

1 Click the **Find** command found in the Editing group on the Home tab on the Ribbon. The Find dialogue box opens, as shown in Figure 7.7.

2 Click the **More** button. The Find and Replace dialogue box expands, as shown in Figure 7.8.

3 Click inside the **Find what** box.

4 Click the **Special** button. The Special menu opens, as shown in Figure 7.10.

5 Choose the option that best describes the non-printing character for which you are searching (i.e. click Tab Character to search for tabs or Paragraph Mark to search for hard returns).

6 Click **Find next**. Word locates and highlights the next occurrence of your specified non-printing character in the document. Click **Find next** again to locate the next occurrence.

7 Click **Cancel** when you've completed searching the document.

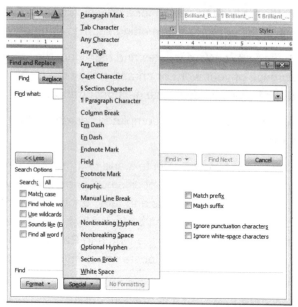

Figure 7.10
The Special menu gives you access to specific non-printing characters such as hard returns, line breaks and tabs.

Timesaver tip

As with most features related to Word, there are handy keyboard shortcuts associated with the Find and Replace features. To open the Find dialogue box, press Ctrl+F. To open the Replace dialogue box, press Ctrl+H.

Once you become comfortable with using all aspects of the Find feature, the Replace feature turns out to be quite innate. And you can access the Replace dialogue box directly from the Find dialogue box – it's just one tab over, as shown in Figure 7.11.

On the Replace tab, you have all of the options you are familiar with on the Find tab. The only difference here is now you have two text boxes to complete. The first is carried over from the Find tab and the second is what you are replacing the first with.

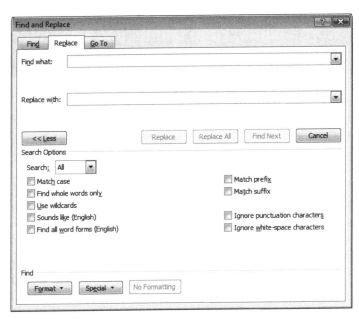

Figure 7.11
Use the Replace dialogue box to locate specific words, phrases or formatting and replace with alternatives.

Additionally, you have the option of searching the document one occurrence at a time and replacing one, several or all occurrences. Or you can replace every occurrence of the Find criteria with the Replace criteria by clicking the Replace All button.

Timesaver tip

While working in the Find and Replace dialogue box, you may have noticed an inconspicuous third tab – **GoTo**. This tab can be used to quickly jump to a new page, section, line, bookmark, comment or footnote in the current document. However, it's even faster to press F5 to open this same dialogue box.

→ Word Counts, Page Counts and Character Counts

Page and word count are always displayed and continuously updated in the lower left corner of your Word window in the Status Bar. Character count is down there as well, it's just slightly hidden.

Automatically and without coercion, every Word document is keeping track (behind the scenes) of the number of words, characters and pages in your document as you type. But, that's not all. Word is also tracking the exact cursor position on the page as well as the line and section number. All of these counts and more can be added to the Status Bar with just one click of the right mouse button. To add document information to the Status Bar, follow these steps:

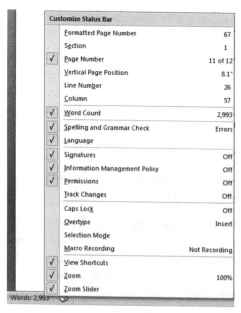

Figure 7.12
Right-clicking the Word Count on the Status Bar opens a shortcut menu with a wealth of document tracking options.

1 **Right-click** the Status Bar. This displays the Status Bar shortcut menu, as shown in Figure 7.12.

2 Click any option without a checkmark to add the indicator to the Status Bar. Click any option with a checkmark to remove the indicator from the Status Bar.

3 When finished, click anywhere on your document to close the Status Bar shortcut menu.

7

Timesaver tip

Word 2007 still offers the familiar Word Count dialogue box, as shown in Figure 7.13. To open the Word Count dialogue box, simply click the Word Count command found in the Proofing group on the Review tab on the Ribbon.

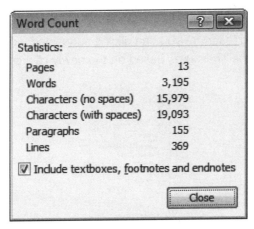

Figure 7.13
Word 2007 still offers the familiar Word Count dialogue box.

→ Using the Thesaurus

The Thesaurus provides synonyms (and the occasional antonym) for words selected in the document. Once the Thesaurus is open, however, you can type any word in the search box to find related synonyms and antonyms.

To use the Thesaurus to find a related word, follow these steps:

1 Highlight the word in the document you are looking up.

2 Click the **Thesaurus** command located in the Proofing group on the Home tab on the Ribbon. This opens the Research task pane, as shown in Figure 7.14.

3 In the Research task pane, you can either select one of the suggested words by clicking the dropdown arrow that appears when you place your mouse over the word and choosing Insert, or you can click a suggested word to search the Thesaurus based on the newly clicked word.

Figure 7.14
Once the Thesaurus is open, you can type any word in the search box to find related synonyms and antonyms.

4 Because the Thesaurus opens in a task pane format, once you've found your new word you can close the Research task pane by clicking the "X" in the upper right corner of the task pane.

Timesaver tip

To open the Thesaurus and search for synonyms for a specific word, simply highlight the word in the document and press the keyboard shortcut combination Shift+F7.

→ Using Microsoft's Research Services

In addition to searching a standard dictionary and thesaurus, Word 2007 offers you access through the Research feature to specific reference books and research sites to expand your word repertoire. With the Research feature, you can choose which reference services Word should include or exclude when providing research services. To choose optional reference books or research sites to search, open the Research task pane (this can be done by opening the Thesaurus or clicking the Research command located in the Proofing group on the Review tab on the Ribbon) and click the dropdown arrow next to Thesaurus, as shown in Figure 7.15.

Figure 7.15
To view optional reference books or research sites to search, click the dropdown arrow next to Thesaurus in the Research task pane.

Furthermore, you can customise the research options by clicking the Research Options link at the bottom of the Research task pane. This link opens the Research Options dialogue box, as shown in Figure 7.16.

In the Research Options dialogue box, simply place checkmarks next to the reference books and research sites you want included in your searches and remove checkmarks from those you would rather exclude from your searches.

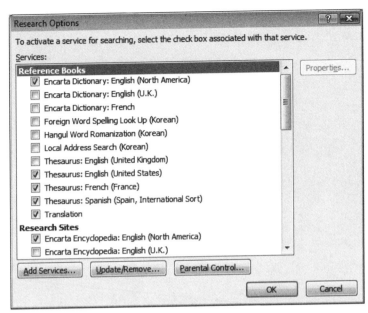

Figure 7.16
You can customise the research options by clicking the Research Options link at the bottom of the Research task pane.

→ Summary

Although performing proofing tasks isn't always the most glamorous of Word tasks, at the very least Word 2007 has made them some of the easiest to perform. With techniques such as Spell Check and Grammar Check, AutoCorrect and Find and Replace, proofreading is now a task you can complete without difficulty. And with tools like the Research Services and related Thesaurus, finding synonyms for over-used words can be an effortless task.

In the next chapter you'll see several options related to the overall setup of your pages, including margins and page orientation. This is also the chapter that covers tabs and indents – a very popular Word topic – as well as working with page breaks and document spacing.

8

Creating Your Page Layout

In previous versions of Word, modifying your page layout could be quite a time-consuming process. To change margins, you could find yourself going in and out of the same dialogue box several times before you achieved the desired effect. But with Word 2007's new results-oriented user interface and live preview features, all things related to page layout have just become worlds easier.

→ Changing Page Orientation

Quite simply, page orientation refers to the direction of your page and Word 2007 offers only two options: portrait or landscape. Pages with portrait orientation print short side by long side (8.5 × 11) while pages with landscape orientation print long side by short side (11 × 8.5). To change page orientation, follow these steps:

1 Click the **Orientation** command located in the Page Setup group on the Page Layout tab on the Ribbon. The Orientation menu displays, as shown in Figure 8.1.

2 Select the desired orientation.

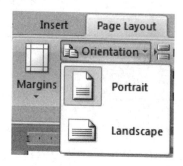

Figure 8.1
The Orientation command displays the two orientation options, portrait and landscape, and is located in the Page Setup group on the Page Layout tab.

Jargon buster

Page orientation refers to the direction of your page and offers only two options – portrait or landscape.

Margins

The margin refers to the amount of space that is left between the document text and the edge of your printed page. In Word 2007, the default margins are set to one inch on all four sides (top, bottom, left and right). However, the Margins command offers several common margin settings. To change the margins using predefined settings, follow these steps:

1 Click the **Margins** command located in the Page Setup group on the Page Layout tab on the Ribbon. The Margins dropdown menu displays, as shown in Figure 8.2.

2 Click the desired margin settings.

> ### Jargon buster
>
> The **margin** refers to the amount of space that is left between the document text and the edge of your printed page.

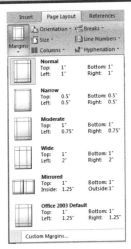

Figure 8.2
The Margins command offers several common margin settings.

In the event that none of the predefined margin settings suits your document requirements, you can choose **Custom Margins** from the Margins dropdown menu. Doing so opens the Page Setup dialogue box, as shown in Figure 8.3. To set custom margins, follow these steps:

1 Click the **Margins** command located in the Page Setup group on the Page Layout tab on the Ribbon. The Margins dropdown menu displays, as shown in Figure 8.2.

2 Click **Custom Margins**. This opens the Page Setup dialogue box, as shown in Figure 8.3.

3 Type in the margin setting for each side (top, bottom, left and right).

4 Click **OK**.

Figure 8.3
Custom margins can be set using the Page Setup dialogue box.

> ## Timesaver tip
>
> The Page Setup dialogue box can also be accessed by clicking the dialogue box launcher arrow found on the lower right corner of the Page Setup group on the Page Layout tab. Other options in the Page Setup group on the Margins tab include page orientation and gutter position (which refers to any area included for binding).

Tabs

By default, tabs are already set on all documents at every ½ inch. To see your tabs, simply look at the ruler bar (located just below the Ribbon). At every ½ inch, below the numbers, you should see small tick marks. Each tick mark represents a default tab stop.

> ## Important
>
> If the ruler bar is not displayed on your screen just below the Ribbon, you can show it by clicking the checkbox next to the Ruler command located in the Show/Hide group on the View tab on the Ribbon.

In fact, you'll notice that every time you press the TAB key the cursor jumps to the nearest ½ inch to the right. If you display the non-printing characters (click the Show/Hide command in the Paragraph group on the Home tab), you'll see tabs in the form of arrows, as shown in Figure 8.4.

Even though Word provides a wealth of tabs, these don't always meet your document requirements. However, you can create your own custom tabs quickly. Each time you add a custom tab stop, any default tab stops set between the left margin and the new custom tab are automatically removed.

Figure 8.4
When non-printing characters are displayed, tabs are shown as small arrows.

It's often easiest to set tabs using the ruler bar and the tab stop indicator (located on the left edge of the Ruler). In most cases, the tab stop indicator displays the left-aligned tab symbol, which resembles the uppercase letter "L". However, if you click the tab stop indicator, you can begin to cycle through the different tab stop options, including Center, Right, Decimal and Bar tabs as well as First-Line and Hanging Indents. To set a tab using the ruler bar, follow these steps:

1 If necessary, select the text for which you are applying the tab.

2 Click the tab stop indicator until you see the indicator for the type of tab you are setting.

3 Click in the ruler bar at the location of the custom tab stop.

4 Repeat Steps 2 and 3 above for additional custom tab stops.

Once custom tab stops have been added to the ruler bar, you'll see tab markers on the ruler bar that indicate the tab stop type, as shown in Figure 8.5.

	1998	1999	2000	2001
West	254	254	635	852
East	254	868	974	214
South	246	595	125	846
North	215	968	485	321|

Figure 8.5

In this figure, note the following tab stops: left tab at 1″, centre tab at 2″, right tab at 3″ and a decimal tab at 4″.

To move a custom tab stop, follow these steps:

1 If necessary, select the text to which you are applying the tab.

2 Drag the custom tab stop to the new location.

To delete a custom tab stop, follow these steps:

1 If necessary, select the text to which you are applying the tab.

2 Drag the custom tab stop down into the document area. This removes the tab from the ruler and deletes it, restoring default tab stops between the deleted tab and the left margin (or closest custom tab to the left).

If you prefer to use a dialogue box for setting tabs, you can find one; it just takes a little bit of digging. To access the Tabs dialogue box, follow these steps:

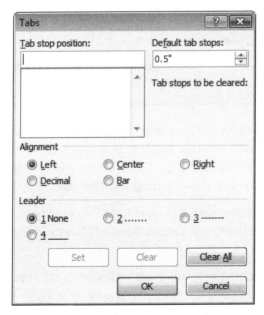

Figure 8.6
You can use the Tabs dialogue box to add or remove custom tab stops.

1 Click the dialogue box launcher arrow on the Paragraph group (found on either the Home tab or the Page Layout tab).

2 Click the **Tabs** button. This displays the Tabs dialogue box, shown in Figure 8.6.

3 Using the Tabs dialogue box, you can add or delete custom tab stops.

→ Working with Indents

Working with indents is one of the most important Word techniques and yet it's often the most misunderstood. Essentially, the indent marks the distance that the paragraph begins or ends in relation to the left or right margin.

Jargon buster

The **indent** marks the distance that the paragraph begins in relation to the left margin or ends in relation to the right margin.

Although you can use the Paragraph dialogue box (opened by clicking the dialogue box launcher arrow located in the lower right corner of the Paragraph group on the Home tab), it's often easier to work with indents using the ruler bar.

Before you create your first indent, you should know the difference between the various types of indents you can create.

To start, all paragraphs have left and right indents set to 0″. You can see the left and right indent markers on the ruler bar represented as triangles, as shown in Figure 8.7.

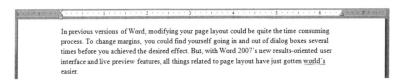

Figure 8.7
By default, all paragraphs have left and right indents set to 0″. The indent markers are represented as triangles on the ruler bar.

Left and right indents are the most common and measure the space between the left or right margin and the beginning or end of the paragraph text. You can view an example of a paragraph with both a left and a right indent in Figure 8.8.

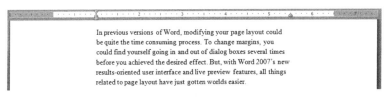

Figure 8.8
This figure has a left indent of 1″ and a right indent of 1″. Note the triangle positions at 1″ and 5.5″ on the ruler bar.

Another possible indent option is a first-line indent. First-line indents indent only the first line of any paragraph a specified distance. In Figure 8.9, you can see a paragraph with a first-line indent of .5″.

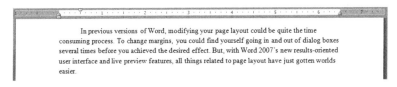

Figure 8.9
This figure has a first-line indent of .5″. Note the top triangle position at .5″ on the ruler bar. The bottom left triangle represents the left indent (at 0″), while the top triangle represents the top line position (at .5″).

Finally, a paragraph can contain a hanging indent. Typically, hanging indents are represented only when working with bulleted or numbered text. A hanging indent occurs when the first line of the paragraph starts closer to the left margin than the remaining paragraph text, as shown in Figure 8.10.

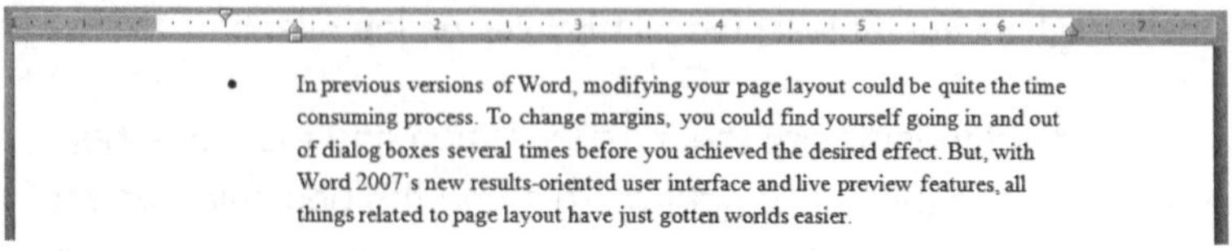

• In previous versions of Word, modifying your page layout could be quite the time consuming process. To change margins, you could find yourself going in and out of dialog boxes several times before you achieved the desired effect. But, with Word 2007's new results-oriented user interface and live preview features, all things related to page layout have just gotten worlds easier.

Figure 8.10
Hanging indents are common when working with bulleted or numbered text. Note the first-line indent marker at .5″ and the subsequent line indent marker at 1″.

Now that you understand the types of indents you can create in Word (left, right, first-line and hanging), you're ready to set paragraph indents. Indents are considering paragraph formatting). As such, it isn't necessary to select a paragraph in order to set an indent (unless you're setting an indent for multiple paragraphs). To set indents for a paragraph, first click inside the paragraph you are modifying, then follow these steps:

■ **To set a left indent**: Drag the rectangle on the ruler bar (under the Subsequent Line Indent marker near the left margin) to the desired indent location.

■ **To set a right indent**: Drag the triangle near the right margin to the desired indent location.

■ **To set a first-line or hanging indent**: Drag the top triangle near the left margin to the desired indent location.

In addition to using the ruler bar and the Paragraph dialogue box to set a left and right indent, you can use the Ribbon. Just switch to the Page Layout tab – here you'll find a different Paragraph group with a left and right indent setting, as shown in Figure 8.11.

8

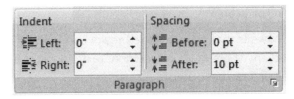

Figure 8.11
You can also use the Paragraph group located on the Page Layout tab in the Ribbon to set left and right indents.

→ Adding Page Breaks

After filling up an entire page with text, Word will automatically create a page break to move you from one page to the next. This is handy. However, these automatic page breaks cannot be deleted. The only way to remove an automatic page break is to insert a manual page break *before* the automatic page break.

In Print Layout View, page breaks are seen easily as the end of one page and the beginning of the next. However, in Draft View, page breaks are a little more inconspicuous, but still fairly easy to locate, as shown in Figure 8.12.

Finally, a paragraph can contain a hanging indent. Typically, hanging indents are only represented with working with bulleted or numbered text. A hanging indent occurs with the first line of the paragraph starts closer to the left margin than the remaining paragraph text as shown in Figure 8-10.

———Page Break———

Figure 8.12
In Draft View, an automatic page break is shown on the top as a simple dotted line. The manual page break is shown on the bottom with the text "page break".

The good news is that manual page breaks can both be inserted and deleted anywhere in your document text. To insert a manual page break, follow these steps:

1 Click in the document where you want the page break.

2 Click the **Breaks** command in the Page Setup group on the Page Layout tab on the Ribbon. This displays the Breaks menu, as shown in Figure 8.13.

3 Choose **Page** from the Breaks menu.

The majority of the options in this menu are section breaks. For more information on section breaks, see Chapter 18.

Timesaver tip

Page breaks can be added quickly by using the keyboard shortcut combination Ctrl+ENTER.

To delete a manual page break, follow these steps:

1 Click at the beginning of the manual page break.

2 Press **Delete** on the keyboard. This deletes the manual page break.

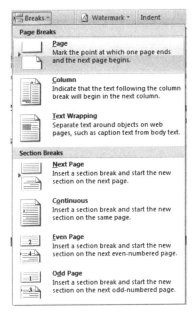

Figure 8.13
Although there are several options listed in the Breaks menu, the only one necessary for inserting a simple page break is the first option – Page.

→ Changing Document Spacing

Two commonly confused subjects are line spacing and paragraph spacing. People often think (mistakenly) that the two are one and the same. They are most definitely not.

Line spacing refers to the amount of space between each line in a document. Line spacing is most commonly set to single- or double-spaced. For an example, see Figure 8.14.

Jargon buster

Line spacing refers to the amount of space between each line in a document. Line spacing is most commonly set to single- or double-spaced.

This text is single-spaced. This text is single-spaced.

This text is double-spaced. This text is double-spaced. This text is double-spaced. This text is double-spaced. This text is double-spaced. This text is double-spaced. This text is double-spaced. This text is double-spaced. This text is double-spaced. This text is double-spaced. This text is double-spaced. This text is double-spaced. This text is double-spaced. This text is double-spaced. This text is double-spaced. This text is double-spaced. This text is double-spaced.

This text is double-spaced. This text is double-spaced. This text is double-spaced.

Figure 8.14
Line spacing refers to the amount of space between each line in a document.

To adjust the line spacing of text in your document, follow these steps:

1 Select the paragraphs you want to modify.

2 Click the **Line Spacing** command located in the Paragraph group on the Home tab on the Ribbon, as shown in Figure 8.15.

3 Select your line spacing option.

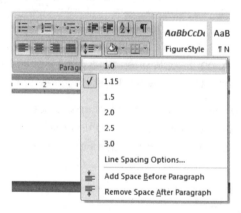

Figure 8.15
You can adjust both line spacing and paragraph spacing from the Line Spacing command. Line spacing options appear at the top of this menu while paragraph spacing options are available below the separator line.

Timesaver tip

To quickly adjust document line spacing, select the affected
paragraphs and press:
Ctrl+1 for single spacing
Ctrl+2 for double spacing
Ctrl+5 for 1½ spacing

Paragraph spacing refers to the amount of space above or
below an entire paragraph and is commonly set to a specific
point size. For an example, see Figure 8.16.

This text has 24 pt paragraph spacing set to below the paragraph. This puts an extra 24 pts of
space after each paragraph return.¶

This text has 24 pt paragraph spacing set to below the paragraph. This puts an extra 24 pts of
space after each paragraph return.¶

This text has 24 pt paragraph spacing set to below the paragraph. This puts an extra 24 pts of
space after each paragraph return.¶

Figure 8.16
Paragraph spacing refers to the amount of space above or below an
entire paragraph.

Jargon buster

Paragraph spacing refers to the amount of space above or below an
entire paragraph and is commonly set to a specific point size.

To adjust the paragraph spacing of text in your document, follow
these steps:

1 Select the paragraphs you want to modify.

2 Click the **Line Spacing** command located in the Paragraph group on the Home tab on the Ribbon, as shown in Figure 8.15.

3 Select **Add (or Remove) Space Before Paragraph** or **Add (or Remove) Space After Paragraph**.

Timesaver tip

To quickly adjust the paragraph spacing of selected text, you can always use the Spacing option located in the Paragraph group on the Page Layout tab, as shown in Figure 8.11.

For options beyond those found on the Line Spacing menu on the Ribbon, you can customise your line and paragraph spacing options in the Paragraph dialogue box, as shown in Figure 8.17.

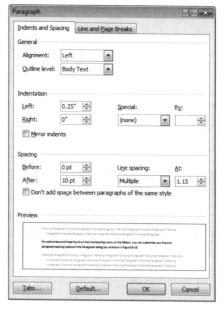

Figure 8.17
For options beyond those found on the Line Spacing menu on the Ribbon, you can customise your line and paragraph spacing options in the Paragraph dialogue box.

You can open the Paragraph dialogue box from a number of locations, but for this particular feature it's often easiest to open it by selecting **Line Spacing Options** from the Line Spacing menu.

→ Summary

In this chapter we covered several crucial page layout elements, many of which you'll use every time you create a Word document. Mastering these techniques is vital to your continued success with Microsoft Word.

8

In the next chapter we'll cover AutoFormatting options, including Themes. AutoFormatting can really take the work out of enhancing your documents.

9

Using AutoFormatting

Brand new to Word 2007 are Themes. Themes are one of the best new additions to this program because they make formatting a document a breeze. As if that weren't enough, Themes are shared among all of the Office 2007 programs, which means you can quickly create a consistent look and feel across all of your Office documents regardless of the program in which they were created.

→ Understanding AutoFormatting

Using Themes allows you to quickly apply uniform formatting to your entire document. Each Theme stores a predefined set of formatting that includes:

- Four text and background colours

- Six accent colours

- Two hyperlink colours

- Two fonts

- Line and fill effects

Word 2007 comes loaded with 20 different Themes from which to choose and format your documents, as shown in Figure 9.1. And, what's more, creating your own Themes is a breeze.

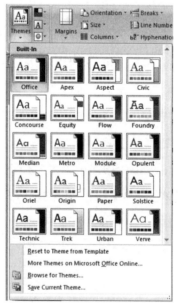

Figure 9.1
Word 2007 comes loaded with 20 different Themes from which to format your documents.

→ Applying AutoFormatting

Each Theme carries a unique name to help distinguish it from another Theme. And to make things easier, Office 2007 shares these Themes. That means, the "Office" Theme in Word holds the same formatting attributes as the "Office" Theme in Outlook. This consistency is going to help you achieve a constant look across your documents.

To apply a predefined Theme to a document, follow these steps:

1 Click the **Themes** command located in the Themes group on the Page Layout tab on the Ribbon. The Themes menu opens, as shown in Figure 9.1.

2 Hover your mouse over each Theme and watch the live preview feature in action.

3 When you locate the Theme you want to apply to the document, click the Theme name once with the left mouse button.

→ Changing AutoFormatting Options

Each Theme consists of three parts:

- Colours

- Fonts

- Effects

Each of these parts can be individually modified to create your own custom Theme or to simply apply individual Theme elements to your document.

Customising Theme Colours

Each Theme contains a set of four text and four background colours in addition to six accent colours and two hyperlink colours. These colours can be individually applied to a document, as shown in Figure 9.2.

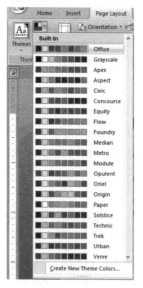

Figure 9.2
Each Theme contains a set of four text and four background colours, six accent colours and two hyperlink colours. These colour sets can be individually applied to a document or customised.

To apply an individual colour set to a document, simply click the Theme Colors command in the Themes group on the Page Layout tab in the Ribbon. However, if you'd like to customise a Theme colour set, follow these steps:

1 Click the **Theme Colors** command in the Themes group on the Page Layout tab in the Ribbon. This opens the Theme Colors menu, as shown in Figure 9.2.

2 Choose **Create New Theme Colors**, located at the bottom of the Theme Colors menu. This opens the Create New Theme Colors dialogue box, as shown in Figure 9.3.

3 Change each colour as desired.

4 Enter a name in the Color Name box.

5 Click **Save**.

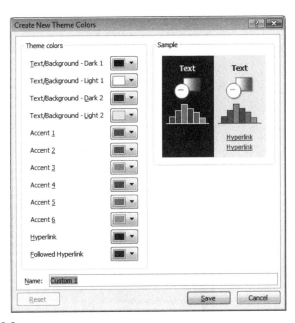

Figure 9.3
To create your own set of Theme colours, customise each colour, enter a name and click Save.

Customising Theme Fonts

Each Theme contains a set of two fonts. These fonts can be individually applied to a document, as shown in Figure 9.4.

To apply an individual font set to a document, simply click the Theme Fonts command in the Themes group on the Page Layout tab in the Ribbon. However, if you'd like to customise a Theme font set, follow these steps:

Figure 9.4
Each Theme contains a set of two fonts. These font sets can be individually applied to a document or customised.

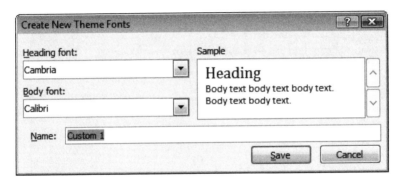

Figure 9.5
To create your own set of Theme fonts, customise each font, enter a name and click Save.

1 Click the **Theme Fonts** command in the Themes group on the Page Layout tab in the Ribbon. This opens the Theme Fonts menu, as shown in Figure 9.4.

2 Choose **Create New Theme Fonts**, located at the bottom of the Theme Fonts menu. This opens the Create New Theme Fonts dialogue box, as shown in Figure 9.5.

3 Change each font as desired.

4 Enter a name in the Font Name box.

5 Click **Save**.

Customising Themes

Although there are 20 predefined Themes that install with the Word 2007 program, you can create your own Themes based on predefined or custom sets of fonts, colours and effects. To create a custom Theme, follow these steps:

1 Apply your desired Theme colour set.

2 Apply your desired Theme font set.

3 Apply your desired Theme effect set.

4 Click the **Themes** command located in the Themes group on the Page Layout tab on the Ribbon. The Themes menu displays, as shown in Figure 9.1.

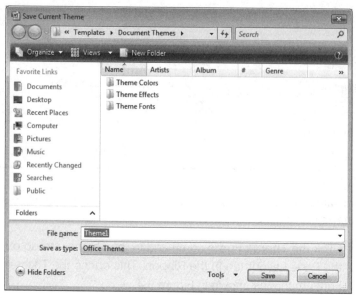

Figure 9.6
Choosing Save Current Theme from the Themes menu opens the
Save Current Theme dialogue box.

5 Choose **Save Current Theme**. This opens the Save Theme
dialogue box, as shown in Figure 9.6.

6 Enter a Theme name and click **Save**.

Custom Themes should be saved in the default Themes folder.
Doing so makes them readily accessible by all Office 2007
programs.

→ Summary

Automatic formatting can certainly save you a great deal of time.
Additionally, Microsoft Office's new Themes help give a
consistent look throughout all of your documents, regardless of
the Office program they were created in.

In the next chapter, you'll learn about AutoText entries and
inserting special characters, symbols and equations.

10

Using AutoText and Special Characters

AutoText was a fan favourite in previous versions of Word. Unlike AutoCorrect, with AutoText you can pick and choose when acronyms and short words or phrases are replaced with longer pieces of formatted text. In Word 2007, AutoText has been incorporated into the new Building Blocks.

You can find much more information about Building Blocks in Chapter 14. However, in this chapter you'll learn how to use the AutoText feature as well as working with special characters, symbols and equations.

→ Understanding AutoText

In Word 2007, the AutoText feature has been integrated with the new Quick Parts feature that resides under Building Blocks. Quick Parts (and Building Blocks) are covered in-depth in Chapter 14. However, you can still use AutoText without a complete understanding of the Building Blocks feature.

Jargon buster

New in Word 2007, **Building Blocks** are sets of Quick Parts (saved items) within a document. These Quick Parts are typically designed to be reused in other documents such as boilerplate company text. Building Blocks and Quick Parts are covered in greater depth in Chapter 14.

AutoText was originally designed as an adjunct to the AutoCorrect feature (AutoCorrect is covered in-depth in Chapter 7). Essentially, when using the AutoCorrect feature, any time you type an AutoCorrect acronym into a document, that acronym is automatically replaced with the word, phrase or symbol you've defined. While AutoCorrect provides a great service for catching commonly misspelled words, it is limited in that you don't have control over when an AutoCorrect acronym is replaced and when it isn't; hence the reason for AutoText.

Jargon buster

With **AutoText**, you can store boilerplate text you use often when creating documents. Unlike AutoCorrect, you have more control with AutoText over when the saved text is inserted into a document.

For example, you may type the same text to close every letter, like this:

Sincerely,

Deanna Reynolds

President

Top of the Line Company

However, an easy-to-remember acronym might be "since" or "closing". The problem with these choices is that "since" and "closing" are both words in their own right. So, if you used either of these words as the acronym in AutoCorrect, you would remove the possibility of ever using them on their own because whenever you type "since" or "closing", Word will automatically replace them with:

Sincerely,

Deanna Reynolds

President

Top of the Line Company

This is where AutoText comes in to rescue you. With AutoText, you can create similar saved entries and name them anything that makes sense, whether your acronym is an actual word or not. That's because, with AutoText, an entry won't be automatically updated unless you press the F3 key after typing the acronym. Now that's flexibility!

You may be asking yourself what types of information are commonly stored as AutoText. Well, here are a few suggestions:

- Company contact information
- Business letter closing

- List of names and addresses

- Pieces of large text you enter on multiple documents

The purpose of AutoText is to save you time in typing and in formatting. So, in order to maximise AutoText, customise it with words and phrases that you use most often.

Timesaver tip

Many transcriptionists use AutoCorrect and AutoText to create a "speed typing" environment by setting up common phrases from their dictation. For example, Internet marketing transcriptionists often type the phrase, "pay-per-click". However, typing hyphens (-) can slow you down. Instead, create an AutoCorrect entry with the acronym "ppc".

→ Creating AutoText Entries

In previous versions of Word, inserting an AutoText entry was as easy as selecting text and clicking the Insert menu. But in Word 2007 the Insert menu has been replaced with the Insert tab on the Ribbon. After a careful search, you have probably discovered that AutoText has been eliminated from the Insert tab because it has been incorporated into the new Building Blocks feature. To create a customised AutoText entry, follow these steps:

1 Select the word or phrase you want to save.

2 Click the **Quick Parts** command located in the Text group on the Insert tab on the Ribbon. This opens the Quick Parts menu, as shown in Figure 10.1.

3 Choose **Save Selection to Quick Parts Gallery**. This opens the Create New Building Block dialogue box, as shown in Figure 10.2.

4 Enter a name for the new AutoText entry.

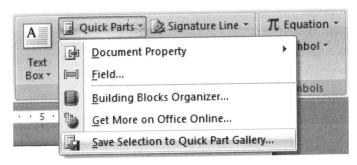

Figure 10.1
Open the Quick Parts menu to access the Save option.

5 Click the **Gallery** dropdown arrow and choose AutoText from the Gallery list. This defines the new Quick Part as an AutoText entry.

6 Click **OK**.

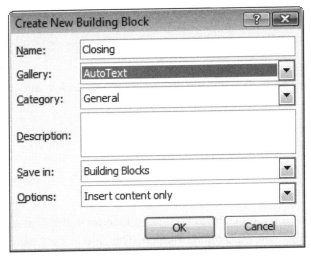

Figure 10.2
In the Create New Building Block dialogue box, enter a name for the new AutoText entry, select AutoText in the Gallery dropdown menu and then click OK.

Inserting AutoText Entries

Custom AutoText entries are stored as part of the Building Blocks feature. As such, you can access your AutoText entries

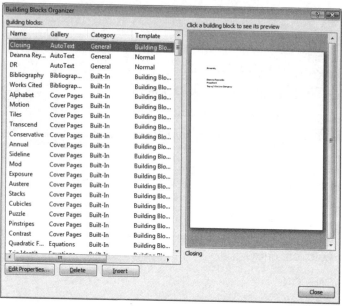

Figure 10.3
The Building Blocks Organizer.

by opening the Building Blocks Organizer, as shown in Figure 10.3.

To insert an AutoText entry using the Building Blocks Organizer, follow these steps:

1 Position your cursor in the document where you want the AutoText entry to display.

2 Click the **Quick Parts** command located in the Text group on the Insert tab on the Ribbon. This opens the Quick Parts menu, as shown in Figure 10.1.

3 Choose **Building Blocks Organizer**. This opens the Building Blocks Organizer, as shown in Figure 10.3.

4 Select the AutoText entry you want to add to the document and click **Insert**.

> **Timesaver tip**
>
> To quickly insert an AutoText entry, type the AutoText entry name and press F3.

Changing AutoText Entries

To change an AutoText entry that's already been saved, it's often easiest to simply recreate the entry, effectively overwriting the old with the new. To change an AutoText entry, follow these steps:

1 Insert the AutoText entry you want to change into the document.

2 Make your desired changes and select the text.

3 Click the **Quick Parts** command located in the Text group on the Insert tab on the Ribbon. This opens the Quick Parts menu as shown in Figure 10.1.

4 Choose **Save Selection to Quick Parts Gallery**. This opens the Create New Building Block dialogue box, as shown in Figure 10.2.

5 Enter a name for the new AutoText entry.

6 Click the **Gallery** dropdown arrow and choose AutoText from the Gallery list. This defines the new Quick Part as an AutoText entry.

7 Click **OK**.

8 When prompted to redefine the existing AutoText entry as shown in Figure 10.4, click **Yes**.

To make creating and adding AutoText entries a little easier, you can add the AutoText command to the Quick Launch toolbar. To do this, follow these steps:

1 Click the **Office Menu** button. This opens the Office menu.

2 Click **Word Options**. This opens the Word Options dialogue box.

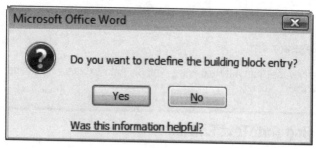

Figure 10.4
When prompted to redefine the existing AutoText entry, click Yes.

3 Click **Customize**. This displays the Quick Launch toolbar customisation options.

4 Under Choose Commands From, select **Commands not in the Ribbon**. This displays a list of commands not available on the Ribbon, including AutoText, as shown in Figure 10.5.

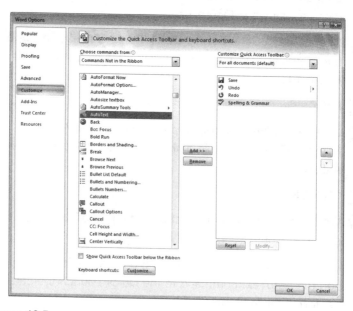

Figure 10.5
Under Choose Commands From, select Commands not in the Ribbon. This displays a list of commands not available on the Ribbon, including AutoText.

5 Select **AutoText**, then click **Add**. This adds the AutoText command to the Quick Launch toolbar.

6 Click **OK**. This closes the Word Options dialogue box.

Once the AutoText command has been added to the Quick Launch toolbar, you can use it to add AutoText entries to your document or create new AutoText entries. To add an AutoText entry to your document using the AutoText command, follow these steps:

1 Position your cursor in the document where you want the AutoText entry to display.

2 Click the **AutoText** command in the Quick Launch toolbar. This displays the AutoText menu, as shown in Figure 10.6.

3 Click the AutoText entry you want to insert.

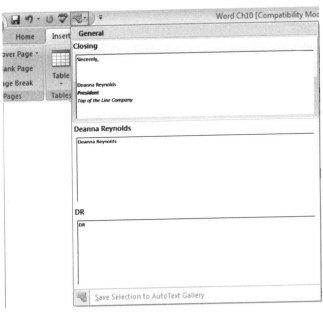

Figure 10.6
Using the AutoText command on the Quick Launch toolbar, you can quickly insert custom AutoText entries into any Word document.

→ Deleting AutoText Entries

Deleting AutoText entries can be done from the same place you add an AutoText entry – the Building Blocks Organizer. To delete an existing AutoText entry, follow these steps:

1 Click the **Quick Parts** command located in the Text group on the Insert tab on the Ribbon. This opens the Quick Parts menu, as shown in Figure 10.1.

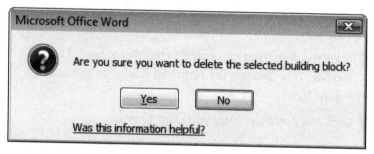

Figure 10.7
When prompted to delete the chosen AutoText entry, click Yes.

2 Choose **Building Blocks Organizer**. This opens the Building Blocks Organizer, as shown in Figure 10.3.

3 Select the AutoText entry you want to delete and click **Delete**.

4 When prompted to delete the AutoText entry as shown in Figure 10.7, click **Yes**.

5 Click **Close**. This closes the Building Blocks Organizer.

→ Using Symbols

For symbols not found on the keyboard, you can use the Symbols command found on the Insert tab. With the Symbols command, you can insert common symbols such as ®, £, ÷, ™ and many more. To insert a common symbol, simply position your cursor in your document and follow these steps:

1 Click the **Symbols** command located in the Symbols group on the Insert tab on the Ribbon. This displays the Symbols menu, as shown in Figure 10.8.

2 Click the symbol you want to insert.

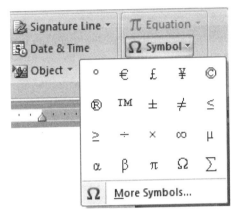

Figure 10.8
Using the Symbols command in the Insert tab, you can access some of the most commonly used symbols.

Jargon buster
Symbols are used for inserting characters such as ®, £, ÷, ™ which are generally not found on a common keyboard.

For symbols not displayed on the Symbols menu, you can open the Symbols dialogue box. From within the Symbols dialogue box, you have access to hundreds of additional symbols specific to each installed font. Some of the symbol fonts include (to name just a few):

- Arrows

- Bullets

- Decorative symbols

To insert any symbol using the Symbol dialogue box, after positioning the cursor in your document follow these steps:

1 Click the **Symbols** command located in the Symbols group on the Insert tab on the Ribbon. This displays the Symbols menu, as shown in Figure 10.8.

2 Choose **More Symbols**. This opens the Symbols dialogue box, shown in Figure 10.9.

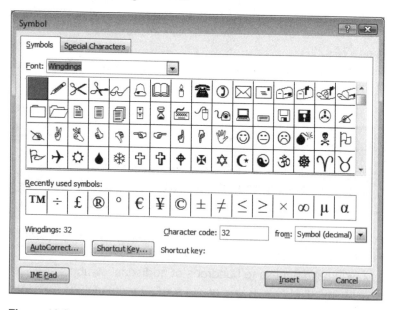

Figure 10.9
Use the Symbols dialogue box to insert any symbol not displayed on the Symbols menu.

3 Change the font to any font of your choosing.

4 Click any symbol and click **Insert**.

5 Click **Close** to shut down the Symbols dialogue box.

Timesaver tip

For commonly used symbols, you can assign a keyboard shortcut combination. Once in the Symbols dialogue box, with your chosen symbol selected, click the Shortcut Key button. Press the keyboard shortcut combination you want to assign to the selected symbol and click Assign. Make sure you don't select a keyboard shortcut combination that is already assigned to another function, such as Ctrl+B for bold.

10

→ Using Special Characters

For characters not typically found in the Symbols dialogue box, you can use the Special Characters tab (see Figure 10.10). Special Characters include, among others:

— Em dash

– Nonbreaking hyphen

¶ Paragraph mark

§ Section symbol

To insert a Special Character, after positioning the cursor in the document follow these steps:

1 Click the **Symbols** command located in the Symbols group on the Insert tab on the Ribbon. This displays the Symbols menu, as shown in Figure 10.8.

2 Choose **More Symbols**. This opens the Symbols dialogue box, shown in Figure 10.9.

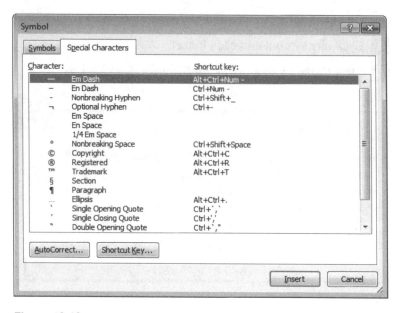

Figure 10.10
Use the Special Characters dialogue box to insert characters such as
a paragraph mark (¶) or an em dash (—).

3 Click the **Special Characters** tab, as shown in Figure 10.10.

4 Click any special character and click **Insert**.

5 Click **Close** to close the Symbols dialogue box.

→ Inserting Equations

An equation is used in Word to display complex mathematical
calculations. You can type an equation in your document or use
the Equation command to insert an equation. When using the
Equation command, you can:

■ Choose from a list of predefined equations.

■ Select and insert symbols using the Ribbon.

Jargon buster

An **equation** is used in Word to display complex mathematical calculations.

To insert a predefined equation, it's often easiest to use the Equation command. To insert a predefined equation, follow these steps:

1 Click the **Equation** command located in the Symbols group on the Insert tab on the Ribbon. This opens the Equation menu, as shown in Figure 10.11.

2 Select one of the built-in equations.

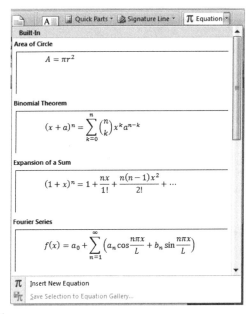

Figure 10.11
Use the Equation command to insert an equation. When using the Equation command, you can choose from a list of predefined equations or create your own using the Equation Tools Design contextual tab.

Writing an equation takes a little more forethought, but is still easily accomplished in Word 2007. To write your own equation, follow these steps:

1 Click the **Equation** command located in the Symbols group on the Insert tab on the Ribbon. This opens the Equation menu, as shown in Figure 10.11.

2 Choose **Insert New Equation**. This opens the Equation Tools Design contextual tab, as shown in Figure 10.12.

3 Use the Equation Tools Design contextual tab to build your custom equation.

Figure 10.12
Use the Equation Tools Design contextual tab to build your custom equation.

Important

When you use the Equation Tools Design Contextual tab to build a custom equation, Word converts the equation into a professionally formatted equation. You can convert the equation to a linear format by clicking the arrow next to a selected equation and selecting Linear from the menu.

If you find yourself using the same equation often, you can add your own custom equations to the built-in equations. To add an equation to the list of frequently used equations, follow these steps:

1 Type and then select the equation that you want to add.

2 Click the **Equation** command located in the Symbols group on the Insert tab on the Ribbon. This opens the Equation menu, as shown in Figure 10.11.

Figure 10.13
In the Create New Building Block dialogue box, enter a name for the
new equation entry, select Equations next to Gallery and click OK.

3 Click **Save Selection to Equation Gallery**. This opens the
Create New Building Block dialogue box, as shown in Figure
10.13.

4 Type a name for the equation.

5 In the Gallery list, click **Equations**.

6 Click **OK**. This closes the Create New Building Block
dialogue box.

Important

Word 2007 supports writing and changing equations created using
previous versions of Word. However, since previous versions of Word
used Microsoft Equation to generate equations, you'll need to use
Equation 3.0 to change those equations.

When using the Equation command, equations are inserted into
the document as a graphic. This graphic can be moved simply
by dragging. However, if you prefer, you can display the equation
inline with the text. To display an equation inline with text, follow
these steps:

1 Click the dropdown arrow next to a selection equation. This displays the equation shortcut menu.

2 Choose **Change to Inline**. This moves the equation to match the paragraph formatting of the closest paragraph.

→ Summary

AutoText, when used properly, can save you time as you generate your Word documents and help ensure a level of document consistency. And with special characters, symbols and equations, you can easily add those sometimes-hard-to-find characters to your pages.

In the next chapter, you'll learn about using both tables and columns to effectively lay out your Word documents.

11

Using Tables and Columns

For lining up text in a Word document, tabs and indents work really well. However, for larger amounts of text, it may be more beneficial to line up your data using either tables or columns. Plus, when using tables and columns, you have formatting and calculation options that aren't available when using tabs and indents.

→ Understanding Tables

Tables provide an easy-to-use method for lining up text in a Word document. Each table consists of a series of columns and rows, as shown in Figure 11.1.

	Column ↓	
		Cell
Row→		

Figure 11.1
A table in Word consists of a series of columns or rows.

To understand how table navigation, selection and data entry work, it's helpful to understand common table terminology.

- **Columns** display vertically. Each table can have as many columns as will comfortably fit within the width of your document page.

- **Rows** display horizontally. Each table can have an unlimited number of rows. However, when the number of rows in a table exceeds the document page length, Word will automatically split the table and create a new table with the same measurements on the next page.

- A **Cell** is the intersection of a row and a column.

Jargon buster

Tables provide an easy-to-use method for lining up text in a Word document. Each table consists of a series of columns and rows.

Working with Table Contextual Tabs

In Word 2007, there are two table-specific contextual tabs to use when working with tables. These tabs will appear only after a table has been created and the cursor is positioned inside the table.

The Tables Tools **Design** contextual tab, shown in Figure 11.2, helps you work with the overall design of your table. On the Design tab, you'll find groups for table styles and borders. You can use the commands in these groups to quickly format your table.

Figure 11.2
On the Design tab, you'll find groups for table styles and borders. You can use the commands in these groups to quickly format your table.

The Tables Tools **Layout** contextual tab, as shown in Figure 11.3, helps you work with the overall layout of your table. On the Layout tab, you'll find groups for working with rows and columns as well as cell size and text and cell alignment.

Figure 11.3
On the Layout tab, you'll find groups for working with rows and columns as well as cell size and text and cell alignment.

→ Creating Tables

In Word 2007, there are several options for creating your tables and the method you choose will depend upon the data already in your document. For instance, you can choose to create a table using text already in the document or you can start from a blank page, add your table and add your text later. If you're an avid Microsoft Office Excel user, you'll be happy to know that you can insert a table into your Word document that resembles an Excel spreadsheet and even gives you access to the Excel Ribbon, directly in Word. Finally, Word 2007 comes with predefined Quick Tables that assist you in quickly adding common tables such as calendars and tabular lists.

Regardless of the type of table you choose to create, you'll always start with the **Table** command located in the Tables group on the Insert tab on the Ribbon. Clicking the Table command opens the Table menu, as shown in Figure 11.4.

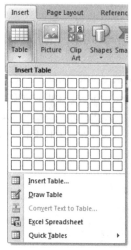

Figure 11.4
Regardless of the type of table you choose to create, you'll always start with the Table command located in the Tables group on the Insert tab on the Ribbon.

Creating a Quick Table

Quick Tables are predefined tables and include:

■ Calendars

■ Double table

■ Matrix

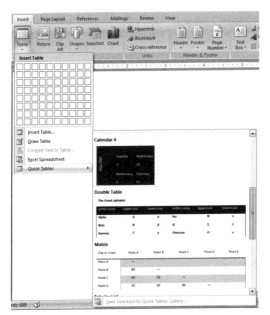

Figure 11.5
Word 2007 comes with predefined Quick Tables that assist you in
quickly adding common tables such as calendars and tabular lists.

■ Tabular list

■ Table with subheadings

To create a Quick Table, first position the cursor in your
document where the table should appear, then follow these
steps:

1 Click the **Table** command located in the Tables group on the
Insert tab on the Ribbon. The Table menu displays, as
shown in Figure 11.4.

2 Choose **Quick Tables**. This opens the Quick Tables menu,
as shown in Figure 11.5.

3 Select your desired Quick Table.

Creating a Table Using Drag & Drop

For those times when you have a specific table need, you'll
probably need to customise it from scratch. In these cases, you

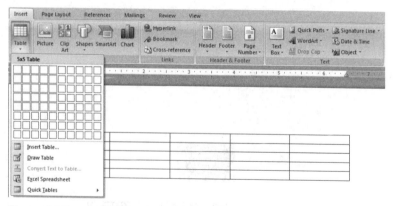

Figure 11.6
By using the drag and drop method to create a table, you can customise your table right from the start by immediately defining the number of columns and rows.

can quickly create a table using a simple drag and drop method. To create a table using the drag and drop method, follow these steps:

1 Click the **Table** command located in the Tables group on the Insert tab on the Ribbon. The Table menu displays, as shown in Figure 11.4.

2 Move your mouse across the grid until the table you are creating contains the appropriate number of columns and rows, then click. A sample table using drag and drop is shown in Figure 11.6.

Inserting a Microsoft Excel Table

If you've ever used Microsoft Office Excel 2007, you know an Excel spreadsheet is laid out in much the same way as a Word table – as a series of rows and columns. Excel's primary purpose is to calculate data. But sometimes you need to calculate data directly in Word. And while Word has some limited calculation capabilities, by inserting an Excel table into a Word document you can perform Excel's advanced calculations right inside Word.

To insert an Excel table into a Word document, follow these steps:

1 Click **Table** command located in the Tables group on the Insert tab on the Ribbon. The Table menu displays, as shown in Figure 11.4.

2 **Choose Excel Spreadsheet**. This opens a new Excel spreadsheet and the Excel Ribbon, as shown in Figure 11.7.

> **Important**
>
> If you choose, you can also create a new table using the Draw Table command. With this technique, you actually draw the outside of your table, then go back through and draw each table row, column and cell divider line. While this can be a time-consuming process, it can be a great way to create a completely customised table. Furthermore, you can create a table from text already entered in your document and separated by tabs. Simply select the text and choose Convert Text to Table from the Tables dropdown menu.

11

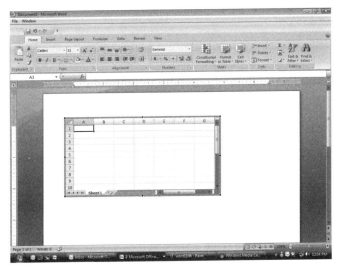

Figure 11.7
By inserting an Excel table into a Word document, you can perform Excel's advanced calculations right inside Word.

→ Working with Data in Tables

Before you can enter your first text in a newly created table, it's helpful to know how to move around a Word table; in other words, navigation. Navigating a table is a little different than navigating a Word paragraph (although, you can type entire paragraphs into a table cell).

Table Navigation and Selection Techniques

Just as mastering the art of document navigation helps you work faster in Word, so can mastering the art of table navigation. To move the cursor inside the table, use these techniques:

To move . . .	Press . . .
Up one cell	Up arrow
Down one cell	Down arrow
Right one cell	TAB or right arrow
Left one cell	Shift+TAB or left arrow
To end of row	End
Beginning of row	Home

You can use either the mouse or the Ribbon to select parts of a table. To select table parts, use these techniques:

To Select . . .	Click . . .
One cell	Click the lower left corner of the cell
Multiple cells	Click and drag across the cells
Row	Double-click the lower left corner of any cell Or Click just outside the left row boundary
Column	Click the top edge of the column
Entire table	Click the Select Table icon displayed in the upper left corner of the table

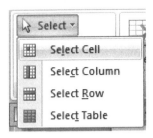

Figure 11.8
You can also use the Ribbon to select parts of a table.

Modifying Table Layout

Typically, inserting and removing columns and rows comes with the territory when working with tables. More than that, however, is the need to occasionally merge two or more cells and split cells as the data you're entering into your table changes. All of these tasks can be easily completed using the Table Tools Layout contextual tab.

Here's an example of a basic table:

East	£400	£500
West	£450	£670
North	£600	£400

Shortly after creating a table, you may find that you need to modify it. For example, you may need to add a row at the beginning for a heading and two rows at the end for additional data or a total. And we haven't even mentioned adding three columns. In Word 2007, modifying the table layout for all of these changes takes only a minute or two. To add columns and rows, follow these steps:

1 Click inside the column (or row) closest to the new column (or row) position. This displays the Table Tools **Layout** and Design contextual tabs.

2 View the **Layout** tab, as shown in Figure 11.3.

3 Click **Insert Above** or **Insert Below** to insert a new row. Click **Insert Left** or **Insert Right** to insert a new column.

Timesaver tip

You can quickly add a row to the end of any table by positioning the cursor in the last cell of the table and pressing TAB.

To remove columns or rows, follow these steps:

1 Click inside the column (or row) you want to delete. This displays the Table Tools Layout and Design contextual tabs.

2 View the **Layout** tab, as shown in Figure 11.3.

3 Click **Delete**. This displays the Delete menu, as show in Figure 11.9.

4 Choose the appropriate delete option.

Figure 11.9
The Delete menu offers a series of delete options.

Timesaver tip

You can use the Cut command to delete selected rows or columns. However, using the Delete key on the keyboard serves only to remove text in a row or column. Using the Delete key on the keyboard will not delete an entire row or column.

11

After modifying our sample table by adding a few rows and columns, here's our table now:

	Qtr 1	Qtr 2	Qtr 3	Qtr 4	Total
East	£400	£500	£460	£650	
North	£600	£400	£550	£300	
South	£700	£350	£250	£900	
West	£450	£670	£900	£450	
Total					

Timesaver tip

You can sort the data in a table by any of the table's columns. To sort a table, simply click inside the table and click the Sort command on the Layout tab. This opens the Sort dialogue box. From the Sort dialogue box, you can choose up to three columns to sort your table by.

The top row in a table is typically reserved for headings. However, a table heading should be centred across the entire table. To achieve this result, you need to merge the table cells. To merge table cells, follow these steps:

1 Select the cells you want to merge.

2 Click the **Merge Cells** command located in the Merge group on the Layout tab.

Important

You can break apart cells by clicking the Split Cells command in the Merge group on the Layout tab. By using the Split Table command, you can break apart a table that runs too long – effectively taking one table and creating two. To break apart a table, simply click in the row that will be the first row in the new (or second) table and click the Split Table command.

After modifying our sample table by merging the top row, here's our table now:

Division Sales					
	Qtr 1	Qtr 2	Qtr 3	Qtr 4	Total
East	£400	£500	£460	£650	
North	£600	£400	£550	£300	
South	£700	£350	£250	£900	
West	£450	£670	£900	£450	
Total					

Timesaver tip

Many common table features are located on the shortcut menu. For example, you can delete, insert and merge all from the shortcut menu. To use the shortcut menu on an existing table, from any selected cell, row or column, simply click the right mouse button.

→ Formatting Tables and Cells

In the previous lesson, you learned how to insert and delete rows and columns, among other tasks. In this lesson, we're going to use the same table example as you learn about formatting.

Division Sales					
	Qtr 1	*Qtr 2*	*Qtr 3*	*Qtr 4*	*Total*
East	£400	£500	£460	£650	
North	£600	£400	£550	£300	
South	£700	£350	£250	£900	
West	£450	£670	£900	£450	
Total					

Clearly, in this example, the columns are way too wide for the data that's displayed. To adjust individual column width, simply position the mouse on the right border of any column and double-click. This automatically fits the column width to the length of the longest text in the given column. However, if you'd like to use AutoFit on the entire table, follow these steps:

1 Click inside the table. This displays the Table Tools Layout and Design contextual tabs.

2 Click the **AutoFit** command located in the Cell Size group on the Layout tab. This opens the AutoFit menu, as shown in Figure 11.10.

Figure 11.10
The AutoFit menu displays a series of choices related to resizing your table.

3 Choose **AutoFit Contents**. This resizes every column in the chosen table to the longest entry in each column.

After using AutoFit, here's our table now:

Division Sales					
	Qtr 1	Qtr 2	Qtr 3	Qtr 4	Total
East	£400	£500	£460	£650	
North	£600	£400	£550	£300	
South	£700	£350	£250	£900	
West	£450	£670	£900	£450	
Total					

In addition to resizing columns and rows, Word 2007 comes with a wealth of table styles. These styles can be used to quickly and easily format your table using text and colour formatting. To apply formatting to a table using a style, follow these steps:

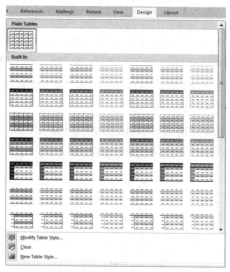

Figure 11.11
The Style Gallery provides a wealth of table styles from which to choose.

1 Click inside the table. This displays the Table Tools Layout and Design contextual tabs.

2 View the **Design** tab.

3 Click the dropdown arrow next to the Style Gallery, shown in Figure 11.11. Choose one of the table styles.

After applying a table style, here's our table now:

Division Sales					
	Qtr 1	Qtr 2	Qtr 3	Qtr 4	Total
East	£400	£500	£460	£650	
North	£600	£400	£550	£300	
South	£700	£350	£250	£900	
West	£450	£670	£900	£450	
Total					

Important

To quickly remove any style applied to a table, click inside the table and choose Clear from the Style Gallery dropdown menu.

→ Adding a Formula to a Table

Although Microsoft Excel 2007 does a terrific job at calculations, occasionally you may need to perform simple calculations in Word. Uncomplicated calculations such as row or column totals can be performed inside any Word table. To insert a calculation inside a table, follow these steps:

1 Click inside the cell that should contain the total. This displays the Table Tools Layout and Design contextual tabs.

2 Click the **Formulas** command located in the Data group on the Layout tab. This displays the Formula dialogue box, as shown in Figure 11.12.

3 Enter your formula. Typical formulas include =SUM(LEFT) where (LEFT) refers to any numbers that appear left of the cursor position in the row and =SUM(ABOVE) where (ABOVE) refers to any numbers that appear above the cursor position in the column. For these formulas, you'll use the actual words "ABOVE" and "LEFT" surrounded by parenthesis.

4 *Optional*: Choose a number format.

5 Click **OK**.

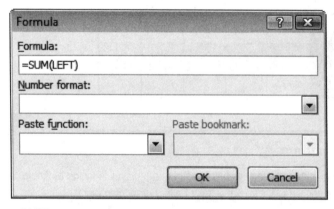

Figure 11.12
Type your formula in the Formula dialogue box. Typical formulas include =SUM(LEFT) and =SUM(ABOVE).

Important

Word formulas are not automatically updated when the related data change. To update a formula to reflect new numbers, you'll need to highlight the formula and update the field by right-clicking and choosing Update Field from the shortcut menu or pressing the F9 key.

After adding formulas, here's our table now:

Division Sales				
Qtr 1	*Qtr 2*	*Qtr 3*	*Qtr 4*	*Total*
East £400	£500	£460	£650	£2010.00
North £600	£400	£550	£300	£1850.00
South £700	£350	£250	£900	£2200.00
West £450	£670	£900	£450	£2470.00
Total £2150.00	£1920.00	£2160.00	£2300.00	£8530.00

Timesaver tip

You can create custom formulas for calculations beyond totalling an entire row or column. For advanced formulas, simply use cell references. For example, use the table below to learn about cell references:

	A	*B*	*C*	*D*
1				
2		B2		
3				
4				

Each column is labelled (behind the scenes) with letters of the alphabet, while each row is labelled (also behind the scenes) with consecutive numbers. Hence, a cell reference uses the corresponding column letter and row number (just like Excel). This means, to create a custom formula that calculates two different cells, simply use the following format: =A1*B3 (where A1 and B3 represent cell references of your choosing).

→ Understanding Columns

Columns are best described as the way text displays in a newspaper, as you can see in the example in Figure 11.13.

When you create columns in Word, two things are happening. The first is obvious. The text is actually formatted into columns, as you can see in the example below. The second, however, happens behind the scenes. In order for Word to display some text that stretches from the left to the right margin and other text broken apart into columns, Word needs to add continuous section breaks above and below the column-formatted text.

Because of this, all text in Word is set to display as one column, by default. So really, when you think about it, all you're doing when you create columns is telling Word to display the text in two or more columns, instead of just one.

The Quick Brown Fox jumped over the lazy dog. The Quick Brown Fox jumped over the lazy dog. The Quick Brown Fox	jumped over the lazy dog. The Quick Brown Fox jumped over the lazy dog. The Quick Brown Fox jumped over the lazy dog.	The Quick Brown Fox jumped over the lazy dog. The Quick Brown Fox jumped over the lazy dog.

Figure 11.13
Text that appears in column format is similar to a newspaper layout.

Jargon buster

Section Breaks allow you to apply different sets of formatting throughout your document. For example, with Section Breaks you can apply different margins to individual pages in your document or display some text as one column while other text displays as multi-columned. Section Breaks are described in detail in Chapter 18.

→ Creating Columns

Once you decide to use columns, the rest is eas
many things related to Word, it's often simpler t
first and format it second. The same is true for columns. To
format text into columns, follow these steps:

1 Type the text that should appear in columns (as well as any
text that should appear before and after the column-
formatted text).

2 Select the text that should appear in a multi-column format.
(Remember, all text is formatted to one column, by default.)

3 Click the **Columns** command located in the Page Setup
group on the Page Layout tab on the Ribbon. This displays
the Columns menu, as shown in Figure 11.14.

11

4 Select the desired column option.

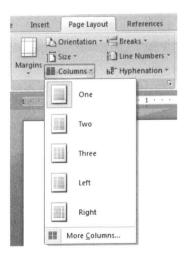

Figure 11.14
Use the Columns command to generate column-formatted text in your
document. However, remember to select the text first and then apply
the column formatting.

Changing and Editing Columns

Modifying text that appears in columns is a fairly straightforward process. But you must remember to always highlight the text you're modifying first. This keeps the section breaks inserted in your document to a minimum.

With columns, you have a few editing options. You can:

■ Insert a line between each column.

■ Change the width of each column.

■ Change the width of the spacing between each column.

Each of these options can be modified by using the Columns dialogue box, as shown in Figure 11.15.

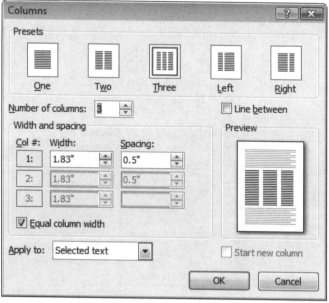

Figure 11.15
By using the Columns dialogue box, you can edit existing columns to include a line between. You can also modify column width and the distance between each column.

Timesaver tip

You can specify where one column ends and the next begins by inserting a column break. Column breaks reside under the Breaks command in the Page Setup group on the Page Layout tab. This is the same place you'll find page breaks.

To modify existing columns, follow these steps:

1 Select the column-formatted text.

2 Click the **Columns** button located in the Page Setup group on the Page Layout tab on the Ribbon. This displays the Columns menu, as shown in Figure 11.14.

3 Click **More Columns**. This displays the Columns dialogue box, as shown in Figure 11.15.

4 Set your column options.

5 Click **OK**. This closes the Columns dialogue box.

11

Timesaver tip

To remove columns, highlight the column-formatted text, click the Columns command and choose **One** from the Columns menu. This sets the text back to the default of one column.

→ Summary

As you can see, tables and columns provide two great options for lining up your text in Word. And there are lots more possibilities in terms of formatting and calculations – possibilities you simply don't see when using tabs and indents.

In the next chapter, you'll work with lists – numbered, bulleted and multilevel.

12

Working with Numbered, Bulleted and Multilevel Lists

Word has several list options, including:

- Bulleted lists
- Numbered lists
- Multilevel lists

Each list has its time and its purpose in your Word document. Of course, determining which list best suits your documents is a task only you can tackle. However, in this chapter you'll learn how to create and customise all three types of lists in Word 2007.

→ Understanding Lists

In Word, when you use bulleted or numbered text, you're actually using a "list". A list can be as simple as to include plain square bullets, as shown below:

- Apples

- Oranges

- Bananas

Or, a list can include consecutively numbered items, as shown below:

1 Apples

2 Oranges

3 Bananas

In both cases, incorporating a list into your document creates hanging indents. (Indents are covered in detail in Chapter 8.) As a result, to adjust the location of the bullet or number character and the space between the character and the text, you simply adjust the indent markers on the ruler bar.

Jargon buster

A **list** is a set of bulleted or numbered text, separated by paragraphs.

At their most complex, lists can be multilevel, as in the outline shown below:

1 Fruit
   a Apples
      i "Eating an apple a day keeps the doctor away."
   b Oranges
      i Oranges are a citrus fruit. Other citrus fruits include lemons and limes.

2 Vegetables

   a Broccoli

   b Carrots

→ Creating Lists

With Word's **AutoFormat As You Type** feature, creating lists in Word is a cinch. To create a bulleted list, position the cursor in the document and click the Bullets command located in the Paragraph group on the Home tab on the Ribbon.

To create a numbered list, position the cursor in the document and click the Numbering command located in the Paragraph group on the Home tab on the Ribbon.

12

Timesaver tip

To quickly create a bulleted list, type an * (asterisk) and press TAB. To quickly create a numbered list, type any number followed by pressing TAB.

Once a list has been started, it can be continued by pressing Enter after the first line of text. When you reach the end of your list, just press Enter twice to discontinue the list character.

Timesaver tip

To add a line in a list without creating a new bullet or number, you can enter a line break by pressing Shift+Enter. Line breaks allow you to drop the cursor down one line without incurring either the list character or any paragraph spacing such as space before and space after. When you're ready to continue the list, simply press ENTER.

→ Changing Lists

Although plain bullets and consecutive numbers get the job done when it comes to lists, there are many more character options. A few of these additional options can be accessed from the Bullets and Numbering commands, as shown in Figures 12.1 and 12.2.

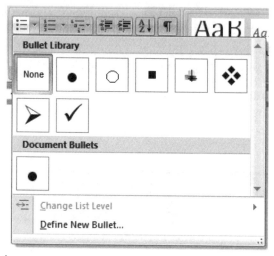

Figure 12.1
Additional common bullet symbols can be accessed by clicking the dropdown arrow next to the Bullets command located in the Paragraph group on the Home tab on the Ribbon.

Timesaver tip

The bullet list character can be formatted by selecting the paragraph mark at the end of each paragraph. For instance, to make a list character bold, select the individual line's paragraph mark and click the Bold command.

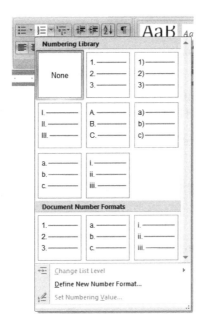

Figure 12.2
Additional common number symbols can be accessed by clicking the dropdown arrow next to the Numbering command located in the Paragraph group on the Home tab on the Ribbon.

For bullet symbols not shown in the Bullets dropdown menu, you can access the Symbols dialogue box through the Bullets command to choose from any number of additional symbols to use as your bullet character. To use an uncommon symbol as a bullet, follow these steps:

1 Either position the cursor in your document or select an existing list.

2 Click the dropdown arrow next to the **Bullets** command located in the Paragraph group on the Home tab in the Ribbon. This displays the Bullets menu, as shown in Figure 12.1.

3 Choose **Define New Bullet**. This opens the Define New Bullet command as shown in Figure 12.3.

4 Do one of the following:

- Click **Bullet** to open the Symbol dialogue box. Choose a font and a bullet character, then click OK.

- Click **Picture** to open the Picture dialogue box. Choose a picture and click OK.

5 Click **OK**. This closes the Define New Bullet dialogue box.

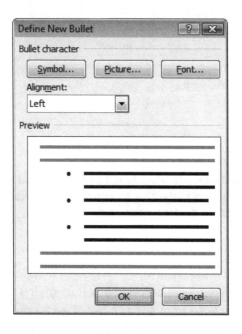

Figure 12.3
Using the Define New Bullet dialogue box, you can choose from a number of symbols and pictures to act as the bullet character for your lists. Additionally, you can format the bullet font from this dialogue box by clicking Font.

For numbered lists not found in the Numbering Library shown on the Numbering dropdown menu, you can set your own numbering format. To define a new numbering format, follow these steps:

1 Either position the cursor in your document or select an existing list.

2 Click the dropdown arrow next to the **Numbering** command located in the Paragraph group on the Home tab in the Ribbon. This displays the Numbering menu, as shown in Figure 12.2.

3 Choose **Define New Number Format**. This opens the dialogue box shown in Figure 12.4.

4 Choose a number style.

5 Choose a number format.

6 Click **OK**.

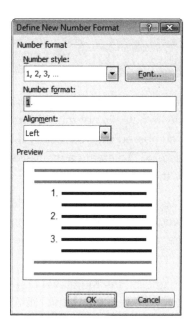

Figure 12.4
Using the Define New Number Format dialogue box, you can choose from several number formats and styles to act as the numbered character for your lists. Additionally, you can format the number font from this dialogue box by clicking Font.

Timesaver tip

When working with numbered lists, you may find that Word tries to connect one list to another even though the two lists may not be located near one another. If this occurs, you can right-click the second list and choose **Restart at 1** from the shortcut menu to start a new numbered list. If, however, Word doesn't connect two seemingly connected lists, using the same shortcut menu choose **Continue Numbering** to continue the second list where the first list left off.

→ Using Multilevel Lists

While multilevel lists appear, on the surface, to be an entirely different animal, they're actually not much more difficult than regular bulleted or numbered lists, especially if you type the text first and format it second. To create a multilevel list out of existing text, follow these steps:

1 Type the list, pressing Tab once for each level. For example, the first level would have zero tabs; second level topics would have one tab; third level would have two tabs: and so on.

2 Select the list and click the **Multilevel List** command located in the Paragraph group on the Home tab on the Ribbon.

Additional Multilevel List options can be found by clicking the dropdown arrow next to the Multilevel List command, as shown in Figure 12.5.

Just as with custom bulleted and numbered lists, you have the option of creating a custom multilevel list as well. To create a custom multilevel list, follow these steps:

1 Either position the cursor in your document or select an existing list.

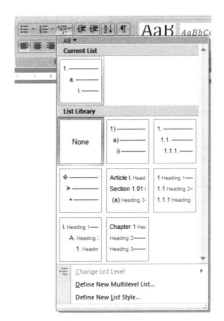

Figure 12.5
Additional multilevel list formats can be accessed by clicking the dropdown arrow next to the Multilevel List command located in the Paragraph group on the Home tab on the Ribbon.

2 Click the dropdown arrow next to the **Multilevel List** command located in the Paragraph group on the Home tab in the Ribbon. This displays the Multilevel List menu, as shown in Figure 12.5.

3 Choose **Define new Multilevel list**. This opens the dialogue box, as shown in Figure 12.6.

4 Choose a level to modify (1–9).

5 Choose a number format.

6 Choose a number style.

7 Repeat Steps 4–6 for each level you want to modify.

8 Click **OK**.

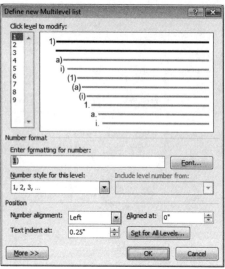

Figure 12.6
Using the Define new Multilevel list dialogue box, you can choose from which level of the multilevel list to format as well as styles and formats.

If you prefer, you can create a multilevel list while you type by following these steps:

1 Position the cursor in your document and choose your desired multilevel list format.

2 Begin entering text.

- To enter text indented one level, press TAB. Continue pressing TAB to indent each level.

- To enter text outdented one level, press Shift+TAB. Continue pressing Shift+TAB for each outdent.

3 When you've finished entering text, press ENTER twice to complete the list.

Often, the easiest way to generate a numbered list is to use the time-saver – start a bulleted list with an asterisk (*) and a numbered list with a number and let Word do the rest. Remember, if Word attempts to make a bulleted or numbered list where there shouldn't be one, you can always press Undo, hit the backspace key on the keyboard or, for a more permanent fix, click the AutoFormat icon that appears next to the newly formatted list and choose Stop Automatically Creating Numbered (Bulleted) Lists.

In the next chapter, you'll learn about everyone's favourite topic – graphics! In Word 2007 the graphics are certainly something to behold as they're bigger and better than ever.

12

13

Adding Graphics to Your Document

Who doesn't love graphics? Well, if you're upgrading from previous versions of Word, there may not have been too much with which you were impressed. But in Word 2007, the new graphics options are definitely making up for lost time. With the new SmartArt capabilities, you can now create stunning graphics to represent your data in very little time. But we're not going to stop there. In this chapter, in addition to exploring SmartArt, we'll look at ClipArt, pictures, charts, WordArt and working with captions.

→ Inserting ClipArt and Pictures

Unless you've been living under a rock, you've probably heard of ClipArt. That's not meant to sound harsh, it's just that most computer users, whether they've been working in a Word environment or not, know, at the very least, what ClipArt is and most likely, how to insert it into a document. In Word 2007, ClipArt hasn't changed drastically from previous versions of Word – that's good news if you're upgrading.

But let's talk briefly about what it means to insert a ClipArt (or other graphic) object into your document. You see, ClipArt images aren't inserted so much as they are embedded. Embedding says that you're placing a copy of an image onto your document. This means that if you modify the image once it's placed on the document, the original doesn't change because there is no link to the source (or original) image.

Jargon buster

Embedding means that you're placing a copy of an image onto your document. This essentially means that if you modify the image once it's placed on the document, the original doesn't change because there is no link to the source (or original) image.

Images you place in Word documents can come from a number of places, including:

- Microsoft ClipArt gallery

- Images saved on your computer

- Royalty-free images downloaded from the Internet

- Any image file, including .gif, .jpg, .tif and .bmp, to name just a few.

Inserting ClipArt

Installed on your computer and available online (with an always-on connection to the Internet such as DSL or cable), you have access to a wealth of ClipArt and Images from Microsoft just by virtue of using Microsoft Office Word 2007. When you search the ClipArt gallery, Word automatically connects to the Internet to bring you the latest and greatest images that match your request. To insert a ClipArt image from the Microsoft ClipArt gallery, follow these steps:

1 Position your cursor where you want the ClipArt image to go.

2 Click the **ClipArt** command located in the Illustrations group on the Insert tab on the Ribbon. This opens the ClipArt task pane, as shown in Figure 13.1.

3 In the Search for box, enter a search term and click **Go**.

4 From the ClipArt results, click any image you want to insert into your document.

Figure 13.1
Use the ClipArt gallery to search and insert ClipArt available on your computer and from Microsoft Online. The ClipArt gallery can be opened by clicking the ClipArt command located in the Illustrations group on the Insert tab on the Ribbon.

Timesaver tip

If you're looking for specific media such as ClipArt, photographs, movies or sound, you can refine your ClipArt search by selecting the appropriate checkboxes under the **Results Should Be** dropdown menu.

Inserting Pictures

Inserting pictures follows a fairly similar process to inserting ClipArt. However, when inserting pictures, Word is looking only on your computer or networked drives for pre-existing images. As a result, you'll notice that instead of working inside a task pane, you'll be working inside a dialogue box to locate the image file you need. To insert a picture into your Word document, follow these steps:

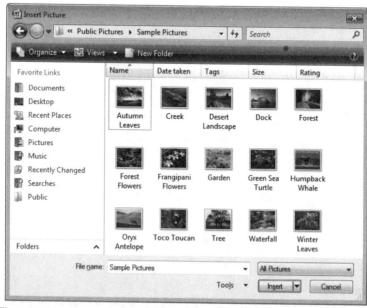

Figure 13.2

Using the Insert Picture dialogue box, you can select an image file stored on your computer or network to insert into your document.

1 Position your cursor where you want the image to go.

2 Click the **Picture** command located in the Illustrations group on the Insert tab on the Ribbon. This opens the **Insert Picture** dialogue box, as shown in Figure 13.2.

3 Navigate to the folder that contains your picture.

4 Select the picture to insert and click **Insert**.

→ Adding a Caption

Jargon buster

Captions are used throughout a document to label images and other inserted graphics. Ultimately, captions can be used to generate a table of figures.

13

Once you begin inserting images of any type into your documents, it's a good idea to label those same images. Any graphic or image in Word can be labelled by using the Caption feature. Captions are used throughout a document to label images and other inserted graphics. Ultimately, captions can be used to generate a table of figures. (For more information on generating a table of figures, see Chapter 18.) To insert a caption, follow these steps:

1 Select the graphic you are captioning.

2 Click the **Insert Caption** command located in the Captions group on the References tab on the Ribbon. This opens the Caption dialogue box, as shown in Figure 13.3.

3 Select a caption label.

4 Select a caption position.

5 Enter the caption text in the top box after the caption label.

6 Click **OK**. This closes the Caption dialogue box and adds the caption to the document.

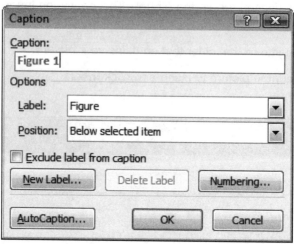

Figure 13.3
In the Caption dialogue box, you can enter the text you want to appear below (or above) any graphic. Captions can be used later to generate a table of figures for the document.

Timesaver tip

To create your own label, once in the Caption dialogue box and click the New Label button. To modify the number formatting of your captions, click the Numbering button.

→ Using SmartArt

SmartArt is new to Word 2007. In fact, SmartArt is available not just in Word but also in Excel 2007, PowerPoint 2007 and Outlook 2007. SmartArt graphics provide stunning visual representations of text- and numeric-based data. And they're easier than any other graphic program to edit, including their colour, presentation and data.

In fact, there are so many choices when it comes to SmartArt (as shown in Figure 13.4), that choosing the type of SmartArt graphic is often the most difficult part of using SmartArt.

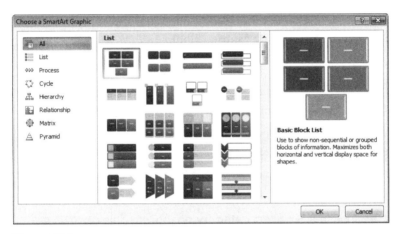

Figure 13.4
The SmartArt Gallery offers seven different categories of stunning graphics you can add to your documents.

About SmartArt Types

There are seven SmartArt categories: List, Process, Cycle, Hierarchy, Relationship, Matrix and Pyramid. Each category defines a specific type of graphic.

When using the **List** type, your main points are highlighted with colourful shapes that emphasise their importance. You should consider using the List layout type when you have data to display that don't necessarily follow a step-by-step process.

The first thing you'll notice about the **Process** type is that each option typically includes arrows to indicate directional flow or specific process steps and their order. In fact, the Process type is the one you'll want to use when creating flow charts.

Just like Process, the **Cycle** layout shows steps in a process. However, with the Cycle layout, those steps are laid out in a circular format.

The **Hierarchy** layout type is best used for organisation charts.

When creating Venn diagrams and radial layouts, use the **Relationship** layout type.

To portray two-dimensional information that highlights fewer than four key points, use the **Matrix** layout.

Finally, for proportional or hierarchical relationships, try the **Pyramid** layout.

As you can see, the options with SmartArt are many. To create a new SmartArt graphic, follow these steps:

1 Click the **SmartArt** command located in the Illustrations group on the Insert tab on the Ribbon. This opens the Smart Art dialogue box, as shown in Figure 13.4.

2 Choose a SmartArt **category** on the left. This narrows the SmartArt types.

3 Choose a SmartArt **type**.

4 Click **OK**.

Timesaver tip

Don't worry too much about picking the perfect layout type in the SmartArt dialogue box. The SmartArt contextual tabs make it easy to change the layout type after the graphic has been created.

Adding Text to a SmartArt Graphic

Once you've created your SmartArt graphic, you'll need to add text to it and the easiest way to do that is with the text pane. To open the SmartArt text pane, follow these steps:

1 Click the SmartArt graphic to select it. This opens the SmartArt contextual tabs.

2 Click the **Text Pane** command located in the Create Graphic group on the Design contextual tab; or click the small arrows located on the left edge of the SmartArt graphic. This opens the text pane, as shown in Figure 13.5.

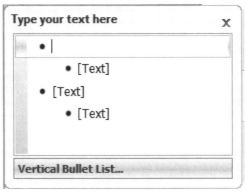

Figure 13.5
Use the SmartArt text pane to add, remove and edit text in any SmartArt graphic. Once you've finished with the graphic's text, you can close the text pane.

Timesaver tip

Deleting bullets from the text pane will remove the related shapes from the SmartArt graphic. And the opposite is true: adding bullets to the text pane will add related shapes to the SmartArt graphic. As an added bonus, working with the bulleted lists in the Text Pane is very similar to working with bulleted lists in a document.

Formatting a SmartArt Graphic

Formatting a SmartArt graphic is in many ways just like formatting any other graphic or Word element. You'll learn more about the contextual tabs used with other graphics later in this chapter.

SmartArt graphics have two contextual tabs you can use to do any necessary formatting: Design and Format.

The **Design** contextual tab, shown in Figure 13.6, can be used to change the SmartArt layout and style in addition to modifying the default graphic colour. This is also the tab that grants you access to opening the text pane and adding new shapes to the existing graphic.

Figure 13.6
Make sure the SmartArt graphic is selected to display the Design contextual tab. On this tab, you can modify everything from the graphic layout to colours and text.

On the **Format** contextual tab, shown in Figure 13.7, you can work with both shape and text styles. Plus, this is where you can modify the size of the SmartArt graphic.

Figure 13.7
Remember, the Format contextual tab will appear only when the SmartArt graphic is selected. Although one of the groups is named "WordArt Styles", you can use the galleries in this group to format the text inside many of the SmartArt graphic shapes.

As you can see, there are many options, not only in choosing a SmartArt graphic but also in modifying any of the layouts you choose.

→ Adding Charts

You probably don't associate charts with Word. But luckily for us, Word has a partner product (Excel) which creates great charts. In Word 2007, Microsoft has done away with the old Microsoft Chart program (thank heavens). This means we can now use the full capabilities of Excel charting directly within Word.

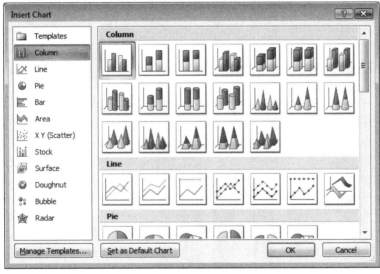

13

Figure 13.8
Clicking the Chart command opens the Insert Chart dialogue box where you can choose from any of the Excel chart options shown.

In fact, you'll notice as you begin to walk through the steps of creating a new chart, the Excel program automatically launches and before you know it, you're using the Word and Excel programs side by side. To create a chart in a Word document, follow these steps:

1 Position the cursor in your document where you want the chart.

2 Click the **Chart** command located in the Illustrations group on the Insert tab on the Ribbon. This opens the Insert Chart dialogue box, as shown in Figure 13.8.

3 Select a chart type and click **OK**.

4 The Word document displays on the left side of your screen. Excel opens and displays on the right side of your screen, as shown in Figure 13.9.

5 Using the Excel window, enter the chart data inside the range outlined in blue. Note that you can expand or shrink the graph data range by dragging the lower right corner of the blue outline. You can navigate the Excel spreadsheet in the same way that you would navigate a Word table. Just make sure you press ENTER after entering each set of data.

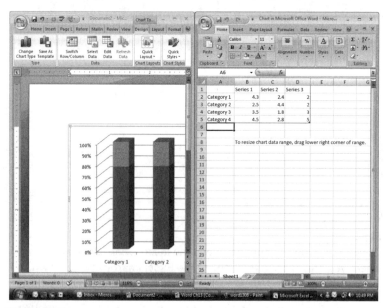

Figure 13.9
Because Word now uses the Microsoft Office Excel program to generate charts, Excel automatically opens and tiles next to Word when you choose to insert a new chart into a Word document.

6 Once you've entered the data, close the Excel window by clicking the "X" in the upper right corner of the Excel window. It isn't necessary to save the Excel spreadsheet. This closes the Excel program and maximises the Word window with the updated chart.

→ Using WordArt

WordArt is no stranger to the Microsoft Word program, and it really hasn't changed much in Word 2007. But that doesn't make it any less remarkable. With WordArt, you can format ordinary text into a stunning graphic object.

Jargon buster

WordArt provides a method for formatting ordinary text into a stunning graphic object.

The WordArt gallery offers approximately 30 different styles from which to choose. Each of these styles can be fully customised with both text and colour, which ultimately leaves the creativity in your hands (if you want it). Of course, WordArt graphics are great without any added formatting. To add a WordArt graphic to a document, follow these steps:

1 Click the **WordArt** command located in the Text group on the Insert tab on the Ribbon. This opens the WordArt gallery. as shown in Figure 13.10.

2 Click one of the WordArt styles. This opens the Edit WordArt Text dialogue box, as shown in Figure 13.11.

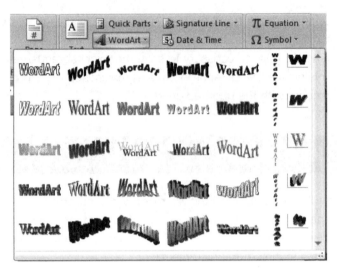

Figure 13.10
The WordArt gallery offers approximately 30 different styles from which to choose. Each of these styles can be fully customised with both text and colour.

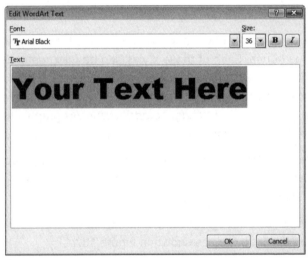

Figure 13.11
Choosing one of the WordArt styles automatically launches the Edit WordArt Text dialogue box. Delete the sample text in this box and add your own, custom text.

3 Delete the sample text displayed in the Edit WordArt Text dialogue box and type your own, custom text.

4 Click **OK**.

Timesaver tip

Don't worry too much about picking the perfect WordArt style. The WordArt contextual tabs make it easy to change the style type after the graphic has been created.

Timesaver tip

You can change the text of any existing WordArt graphic by double-clicking the graphic. This action opens the Edit WordArt Text dialogue box.

13

→ Changing the Appearance of Graphics

Whenever you create or insert graphics in Word, new contextual tabs open designed solely for working with graphics. Although these tabs vary slightly in their commands depending upon the type of graphic that you're working on, the purpose of each remains the same.

Depending on the type of graphic you're working on, you may see one, two or three contextual tabs:

■ Design

■ Format

■ Layout

Design

The Design contextual tab typically holds groups for modifying styles and colours. In many cases, this is also the tab you'll want to use for finding the command that allows you to edit any text on the graphic.

Figures 13.12 and 13.13 illustrate two different versions of the Design contextual tab as shown when working with SmartArt and charts.

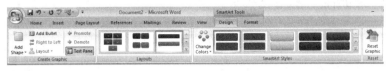

Figure 13.12
When working with SmartArt graphics, the SmartArt Tools Design contextual tab is available. On this tab, you have access to working with SmartArt text, layouts and styles.

Figure 13.13
When working with charts, the Chart Tools Design contextual tab is available. On this tab, you have access to working with chart data, layouts and styles.

Format

The Format contextual tab is the one tab that you'll see when working with every graphic object, including:

- ClipArt and Pictures
- SmartArt
- Charts
- WordArt

The Format contextual tab, although varying a little with each graphic type, typically holds groups for arranging graphics as well as modifying the shape outline, fill, effects and size.

Figures 13.14–13.17 illustrate four different versions of the Format contextual tab as shown when working with ClipArt and Pictures, SmartArt, Charts and WordArt.

Figure 13.14
When working with ClipArt and images, the Picture Tools Format contextual tab is available. On this tab, you have access to working with picture styles and picture editing tools such as brightness and contrast.

Figure 13.15
When working with SmartArt, the SmartArt Tools Format contextual tab is available. On this tab, you have access to working with overall SmartArt shape styles as well as individual shape text formatting.

Figure 13.16
When working with charts, the Chart Tools Format contextual tab is available. On this tab, you have access to working with individual chart components in the Current Selection group as well as chart placement options in the Arrange group.

Figure 13.17
When working with WordArt, the WordArt Tools Format contextual tab is available. On this tab, you have access to working with every formatting feature available to WordArt. When you create and edit WordArt, the Format contextual tab is the only tab specific to WordArt that is available.

Layout

Only one graphic type displays the Layout contextual tab – charts. This tabs holds groups for working with specific chart elements such as labels and backgrounds.

Figure 13.18 illustrates the Layout contextual tab as shown when working with charts.

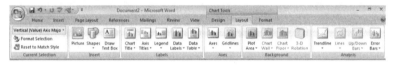

Figure 13.18
When working with charts, the Chart Tools Layout contextual tab is available. On this tab, you have access to working with specific chart elements such as labels and backgrounds.

→ Summary

Aren't graphics fun? By adding graphics to your documents, you can take page after page of straight (and sometimes boring) text and turn it into a visual masterpiece that draws and keeps the reader's attention.

In the next chapter, you'll learn about the new Quick Parts in Word 2007. Quick Parts are stored sets of formatted text that make setting up new documents a breeze. You've already learned a little about Quick Parts (and Building Blocks) in Chapter 10. However, in the next chapter we'll explore the different types of Quick Parts you can create and add to your documents.

14

Using Building Blocks and Quick Parts

In Word 2007, the Building Blocks feature and related Quick Parts are getting a lot of use. In fact, you've already learned about a few Quick Parts in this book, including AutoText, watermarks, quick tables and cover pages.

Each of these Building Blocks contains sets of Quick Parts (saved items) within a document. These Quick Parts are typically designed to be reused in other documents such as boilerplate company text.

→ Understanding Building Blocks and Quick Parts

Building Blocks are reusable pieces of content or other document parts that are stored in galleries. You can access and reuse the building blocks at any time. You can also save building blocks and distribute them with templates so that others can use the building blocks you created.

Jargon buster

New in Word 2007, **Building Blocks** are sets of predefined Quick Parts (saved items) within a document. These items are typically designed to be reused in other documents and include things like boilerplate company text or a privacy statement as well as graphics and formatting.

Beyond simple boilerplate text, Word 2007 offers Building Blocks which allow you to add frequently used content to your documents. Word's Building Blocks feature comes loaded with a predefined gallery, including:

- Cover pages
- Pull quotes
- Headers and footers

Beyond the predefined Building Blocks, you can also create your own Quick Parts. You learned about creating AutoText Quick Parts in Chapter 10. But there are several other areas of Word's Quick Parts that you can customise. For example, you can use Quick Parts to:

- Simplify the addition of custom text, such as legal disclaimer text.

- Store a company logo with a text-based slogan.

- Streamline documents with company-wide formatting for headers, footers and text boxes.

One of the truly remarkable features of these customisable Building Blocks is that they are pretty smart as well. For instance, one Building Block type is a cover page. When you add a cover page, regardless of your cursor position in the document, it is automatically added at the beginning of the document. Header Building Blocks instinctively know to display in the header area, while Textbox Building Blocks are inserted in the document at the cursor page location.

Jargon buster

Quick Parts are any Building Block parts that you, the user, customise.

Overall, Building Blocks are inclusive bits of content and can be:

14

- Cover pages

- Headers

- Footers

- Page numbers

- Text boxes

- Equations

- Tables of contents

- Bibliographies

- Watermarks

Quick Parts are any parts that you, the user, customise.

→ Creating Quick Parts

Predefined Building Blocks can be found on the following tabs:

- Insert
  - → Cover page
  - → Quick tables
  - → Page number
  - → Header
  - → Footer
  - → Text box
  - → Equation
- Page layout
  - → Watermark
- References
  - → Table of contents
  - → Bibliography

Apart from using the predefined Building Blocks, you can create your own Quick Parts based on custom content. To create a custom Quick Part, follow these steps:

1 Select the content you want to save.

2 Click the **Quick Parts** command located in the Text group on the Insert tab on the Ribbon. This opens the Quick Parts menu.

3 Choose **Save Selection to Quick Parts Gallery**. This opens the Create New Building Block dialogue box, as shown in Figure 14.1.

4 Enter a name for the new Quick Part.

5 Click **OK**.

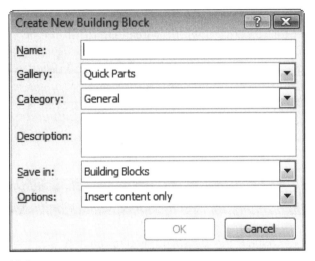

Figure 14.1
In the Create New Building Block dialogue box, enter a name for the new Quick Part entry, select the Quick Part type next to Gallery and then click OK.

Important

When selecting content to save as a Quick Part, you can include text, images and special formatting. This means, whatever you choose to save as a Building Block will be inserted into your documents exactly as it appears when you select it for saving, including any images, hyperlinks, text and formatting.

When saving new Quick Parts, it's important to point out that you don't have to choose "Quick Parts" as the Building Block gallery. You can save to other galleries (as you saw in Chapter 10 when you learned how to create a new AutoText entry) as well.

Important

By default, Word stores Quick Parts in the Building Blocks.dotx template. This is the file where all built-in content is stored. However, you can also choose to put the Building Blocks in your Normal template or into any other specific template. If you begin to receive error messages related to your Building Blocks file (if they occur, they typically pop up when you are exiting Word), one known fix is to search your computer for the Building Blocks.dotx file and delete it. This way, the next time you launch Word, your default Building Blocks will be restored and the error message will stop. Doing so, however, will also delete any Quick Parts you've created and saved in the Building Blocks template.

→ Adding Quick Parts to Your Document

Once your Quick Parts are saved, you're ready to add them to your documents. Because Quick Parts are stored in the Building Blocks.dotx template, they immediately become available to all new documents. To add a Quick Part to your document, follow these steps:

1 Position the cursor in your document where you want to add the Quick Part.

2 Click the **Quick Parts** command located in the Text group on the Insert tab on the Ribbon. This opens the Quick Parts menu shown in Figure 14.2 with a list of newly added Quick Parts.

3 Click the part you want to insert.

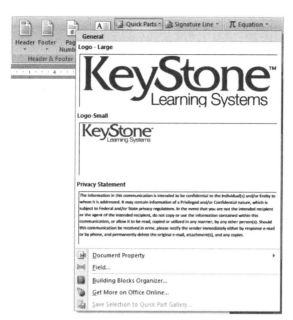

Figure 14.2
Use the Quick Parts dropdown menu to quickly add saved Quick Parts to any document.

You can see all of the available Building Blocks and Quick Parts by opening the Building Blocks Organizer (located on the Quick Parts dropdown menu). Additionally, by using the Building Blocks Organizer, you can preview, edit or delete building blocks and, if you choose, insert them in your current document.

Timesaver tip

Over time, the Building Blocks Organizer may become a crowded place with all of the predefined Building Blocks and customised Quick Parts. However, you can delete Building Blocks and Quick Parts you no longer use from the Building Blocks Organizer. Simply open the Building Blocks Organizer, click the name of the entry and choose Delete. This won't remove the deleted Building Block from any document in which it already resides, but it will remove the option of using that Building Block in future documents.

→ Changing Quick Parts

The only way to change a Quick Part is to replace it with new content, saved under the old name. To change a Quick Part, follow these steps:

1 Insert the Quick Part into a document and make your desired changes.

2 Select the Quick Part entry and click the **Quick Parts** command located in the Text group on the Insert tab on the Ribbon. This opens the Quick Parts menu.

3 Choose **Save Selection to Quick Part Gallery**. This opens the Create New Building Block dialogue box, as shown in Figure 14.1.

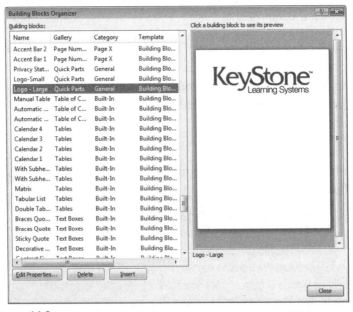

Figure 14.3
Use the Building Blocks Organizer to view, edit and delete your Quick Parts.

4 Type the original Quick Part name, being sure to select the same category and gallery.

5 Click **OK**.

6 When prompted to redefine the Building Block entry, click **Yes**.

You can also choose to just rename an existing Quick Part to something more meaningful to your work. To rename a Quick Part, follow these steps:

1 Click the **Quick Parts** command located in the Text group on the Insert tab on the Ribbon. This opens the Quick Parts menu.

2 Click **Building Blocks Organizer**. This opens the Building Blocks Organizer as shown in Figure 14.3.

3 Click the Quick Part entry that you want to rename.

4 Click **Edit Properties**. This opens the Modify Building Block dialogue box, as shown in Figure 14.4.

5 Type a new name and click **OK**.

14

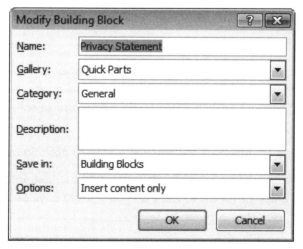

Figure 14.4
Using the Modify Building Block dialogue box, you can modify the name, gallery and category of selected Quick Parts.

6 When prompted to redefine the Building Block entry, click **Yes**.

Timesaver tip

When working with the Building Block Organizer, you can sort the Building Blocks list by clicking any of the column headers at the top of the dialogue box. For example, to group together all of the custom Quick Parts, click the Gallery column heading.

→ Sharing Quick Parts with Others

Having Quick Parts for your personal use is a great benefit. However, being able to share your Quick Parts with others is an even bigger bonus. Since Quick Parts are stored in a template (Remember? Building Blocks.dotx.), you can actually save them in your custom templates. This means, all you need to do to share your Quick Parts is to save them in a template you create and then send that custom template to those you're sharing with. To share Quick Parts with others, follow these steps:

1 Create a new, blank Word document.

2 From the Office menu, point to **Save As,** then choose **Word Template** from the Save As submenu. This opens the Save As dialogue box with Word Template already selected as the file type.

3 Type a file name for the new template and click **Save**.

4 With the custom template still open, add the text, formatting and graphics for the Quick Part you want to save and select the Quick Part entry text.

5 Click the **Quick Parts** command located in the Text group on the Insert tab on the Ribbon. This opens the Quick Parts menu.

6 Choose **Save Selection to Quick Part Gallery**. This opens the Create New Building Block dialogue box, as shown in Figure 14.1.

7 Type a Quick Part name.

8 From the Save in dropdown menu, choose the name of your custom template (the document that is currently open). An example is shown in Figure 14.5.

9 Click **OK**.

10 **Delete** the Quick Part entry in the document (not in the Building Blocks Organizer).

11 Repeat Steps 4–10 for additional Quick Parts you want to add to the template to share with others.

12 Send the template to others.

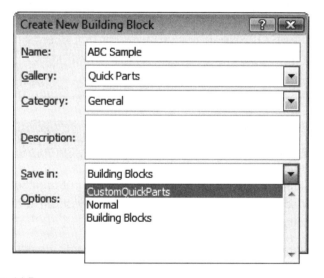

Figure 14.5
Be sure to choose the name of the open template for the Save in location. This ensures that the new Quick Part will be transferred to the new user with the template.

Timesaver tip

If you have existing Quick Parts you want to share, create a new, blank Word template. With this template open, display the Building Blocks Organizer. For each Quick Part you want to share, you can select it and then click Edit Properties. Once in the Edit Properties dialogue box, you can choose to save the Quick Part in the new template. This moves the Quick Part to the new template and takes it out of the Building Blocks template.

Important

When the people you've sent the customised template to save the template file, be sure they save it to the **Application Data** folder. Doing so allows the Building Blocks that you saved with the template to be available in their Building Blocks galleries and in their Building Blocks Organizer. To quickly locate the Application Data folder, tell the user to open the Start menu and type "appdata" in the Start menu search field on Windows Vista.

→ Summary

With a little practice, Quick Parts can help you put together streamlined documents that you find personally pleasing or that match company document guidelines.

In the next chapter, you'll learn about adding other elements (some of them Building Blocks) to your documents as we cover headers, footers, page numbers, endnotes, footnotes and citations.

15

Adding Headers, Footers and Other References

In this chapter, you'll learn about several document features that will add that final touch of polish, such as page numbers, endnotes, footnotes and citations.

Elements such as these are often a required part of many documents. This makes using them critical to the success of many Word users. Fortunately, in Word 2007, inserting and editing these elements is pretty straightforward.

→ Using Headers and Footers

Any text or graphics that appear inside the top and bottom margins of a document fall under the category of header and footer. Headers appear at the top of each document page, typically within the first half inch of the paper. Footers appear at the bottom of each document page, typically within the last half inch of the paper. See Figure 15.1 for a sample, predefined header.

Figure 15.1
Word 2007 comes loaded with several predefined headers (and footers). This image provides just one example.

Jargon buster

A **header** (top) and **footer** (bottom) includes any text or graphics that appear on a page, typically within half an inch of the edge of the paper. Headers and footers can be the same throughout all pages in a document or, with the right settings, can change with each page.

To make headers and footers even more user-friendly, they have been incorporated into Word 2007's new Building Blocks. (Using Building Blocks and Quick Parts is discussed in detail in Chapter 14.) For the user, these Building Blocks make adding headers and footers to a document tremendously simple. To add a predefined header, follow these steps:

1 Click the **Header** command located in the Header and Footer group on the Insert tab on the Ribbon. This displays the Header Gallery shown in Figure 15.2.

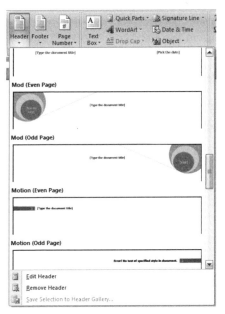

Figure 15.2
Use the Header gallery to choose a preformatted header for your document. Headers and footers are given unique names which allows you to choose each independently, still ensuring continuity in your document.

2 Click the header style of your choice.

3 Edit the header text, as desired.

4 Click the **Close Header and Footer** command located in the Close group on the Header and Footer Design contextual tab.

To add a predefined footer, follow these steps:

1 Click the **Footer** command located in the Header & Footer group on the Insert tab on the Ribbon. This displays the Footer gallery, shown in Figure 15.3.

2 Click the footer style of your choice.

3 Edit the footer text, as desired.

4 Click the **Close Header & Footer** command located in the Close group on the Header & Footer Design contextual tab.

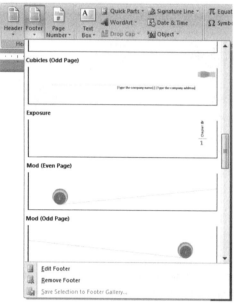

Figure 15.3
Use the Footer gallery to choose a preformatted footer for your document.

Timesaver tip

Once a header and footer have been created, you can quickly access them again for editing by double-clicking the greyed out header (or footer) text. Doing so activates the Header and Footer Design contextual tab and drops the cursor into the header (or footer) for editing. Likewise, you can close the header and footer view by double-clicking outside of the header and footer area on the open document.

However, you aren't limited to the predefined headers and footers – you can use your own creativity to create a custom header or footer. Whether you choose to use a header or footer Building Block or build your own header or footer, you can further customise your addition(s) using the Header & Footer Design contextual tab shown in Figure 15.4.

Figure 15.4
When you are editing a header or footer, use the Header & Footer Design contextual tab to work directly with features within the context of the inserted header and/or footer.

Using the Header & Footer Design contextual tab, you can insert elements, such as:

- Date and Time
- Pictures
- ClipArt
- Page numbers

Timesaver tip

Existing headers and footers can be removed simply by clicking the Header (or Footer) command on the Insert tab and choosing Remove from the dropdown menu.

15

Odd and Even Headers and Footers

Often, you'll want to show one header on odd pages and a different header on even pages. A good example of this is a manual or a book. Many books have the title on the left-hand page (or, even page) and the current chapter heading on the right-hand page (or, odd pages), or vice versa. Or maybe you'd prefer to have one header or footer on page one and a different header or footer on the remaining pages in the document.

Each of these scenarios can be achieved by using the checkboxes located in the Options group on the Header and

Footer Design contextual tab. To set different headers and footers throughout a document, follow these steps:

1 View the header (or footer) in edit mode by clicking the **Header** (or footer) command located in the Header and Footer group on the Insert tab on the Ribbon. This displays the Header (or Footer) dropdown menu.

2 Choose **Edit Header** (or Edit Footer). This positions the cursor in the closest header (or footer) and displays the Header and Footer Design contextual tab.

3 Choose to enable or display the following options:

- Different First Page

- Different Odd & Even Pages

4 Click the **Close Header and Footer** command located in the Close group on the Header and Footer Design contextual tab.

Timesaver tip

You can move quickly between headers and footers by using the commands located in the Navigation group on the Header and Footer Design contextual tab.

→ Adding Page Numbers

Just like headers and footers, page numbers are integrated with the new Building Blocks in Word 2007. There are several predefined page numbers from which to choose, as you can see in Figure 15.5.

To add a page number to a document, follow these steps:

1 Click the **Page Number** command located in the Header and Footer group on the Insert tab on the Ribbon. This displays the Page Number gallery, as shown in Figure 15.5.

Figure 15.5
Page number Building Blocks offer the most predefined options of all of the available Word 2007 Building Blocks.

2 Hover the mouse over the page number position you want. A submenu appears.

3 Click the page number style from the submenu gallery.

Timesaver tip

To insert a page number not located at the top or bottom of the page, you can choose to insert a page number at the "**current position**". This inserts a page number at the cursor position rather than along the top or bottom edge.

Once a page number is inserted, you may need to modify the starting number. Page numbers always fall consecutively based on the first number. There isn't a whole lot you can change about page numbers and how they increment, but you can modify the first page number. And you can set page numbering to different parameters in each section within a document. (Using sections is covered in detail in Chapter 18.) To modify the starting page number for a document, follow these steps:

1 Select the page number in the document.

2 Click the **Page Number** command located in the Header and Footer group on the Insert tab on the Ribbon. This opens the Page Number dropdown menu, shown in Figure 15.5.

3 Choose **Format Page Numbers**. This opens the Page Number Format dialogue box shown in Figure 15.6.

4 In the Start At box, enter the starting page number of your choosing.

5 Click **OK**. This closes the Page Number Format dialogue box.

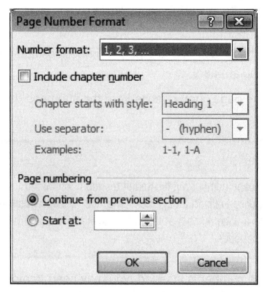

Figure 15.6
Use the Page Number Format dialogue box to modify the starting number for page numbers in a document.

→ Adding Endnotes and Footnotes

Footnotes and endnotes are often used by people writing
research papers to explain text references or document sources.
Endnotes are references that print at the end of a document and
explain text in a document, while footnotes are references that
print at the bottom of each page and explain marked text located
on the same page.

Jargon buster

Endnotes are references that print at the end of a document and
explain text in a document.

Jargon buster

Footnotes are references that print at the bottom of each page and
explain marked text located on the same page.

15

To make it easy, footnotes and endnotes are edited in the same
dialogue box. Since footnotes and endnotes are used to
reference text, it makes it even easier to locate the command on
the Ribbon – both commands are found in the Footnotes group
on the References tab.

To insert an endnote, follow these steps:

1 Position the cursor in the document where you want the
endnote reference number to display.

2 Click the **Endnote** command located in the Footnotes group
on the References tab on the Ribbon. This inserts a
reference in the text at the cursor location and a reference at
the end of the document (see Figure 15.7).

3 Type the endnote text.

Adding Endnotes and Footnotes

Footnotes[i] and Endnotes are often used by people writing research papers to explain text references or document sources. Endnotes are references that print at the end of a document that explain text in a document; while, Footnotes are references that print at the bottom of each page and explain marked text located on the same page.

---

[i] Sample Endnote text goes here

Figure 15.7
Endnotes are references that print at the end of a document that explain text in a document.

Timesaver tip

After inserting either a footnote or an endnote, you can quickly see the related footnote or endnote text by hovering the mouse over the number reference located in the document text.

To insert a footnote, follow these steps:

1 Position the cursor in the document where you want the footnote reference number to display.

2 Click the **Footnote** command located in the Footnotes group on the References tab on the Ribbon. This inserts a reference in the text at the cursor location and a reference at the end of the document.

3 Type the footnote text (see Figure 15.8).

In addition to the individual commands located on the Ribbon, you can insert (and modify) both endnotes and footnotes using the Footnote and Endnote dialogue box. You can open the Footnote and Endnote dialogue box shown in Figure 15.9, by clicking the dialogue box launcher located in the lower right corner of the Footnotes group.

Adding Endnotes and Footnotes

Footnotes[1] and Endnotes are often used by people writing research papers to explain text references or document sources. Endnotes are references that print at the end of a document that explain text in a document; while, Footnotes are references that print at the bottom of each page and explain marked text located on the same page.

[1] Sample Footnote text goes here|

Figure 15.8
Footnotes are references that print at the bottom of each page and explain marked text located on the same page.

Figure 15.9
The Footnote and Endnote dialogue box can be opened by clicking the dialogue box launcher arrow located in the lower right corner of the Footnotes group located on the References tab on the Ribbon.

Timesaver tip

Footnotes and endnotes can be deleted from the document simply by deleting the superscript footnote reference number that displays within the document text. Deleting the reference number will automatically delete the associated text displayed either at the bottom of the page or at the end of the document.

→ Inserting Citations

In Word 2007, citations and bibliographies go hand in hand. A bibliography, of course, is a list of sources you consulted while creating your document. Typically, bibliographies are added at the end of a document. However, in order to use Word to automatically build a bibliography, you'll need to mark citations and generate sources that Word can refer to.

Jargon buster

A **bibliography** is a list of sources you consulted while creating your document.

Jargon buster

A **citation** is a group of information such as author, title, pagination and dates which identifies an item – book, journal article, or other format (University of Connecticut Libraries, 2006). Citations should include enough information for one to be able to locate the original item.

Timesaver tip

Any time you create a new source, Word saves the source information. This way, you can find and use any source you have created.

Important

You can change your citation and source style by clicking the Style dropdown arrow located in the Citations & Bibliography group on the References tab on the Ribbon. **This should be done before you create your first citation**.

Luckily for us, whenever we create a citation, Word reminds us to create a matching source. To add a citation and a source to a document, follow these steps:

1 Position the cursor in your document at the end of the text you are citing.

2 Click the **Insert Citation** command located in the Citations & Bibliography group on the References tab on the Ribbon. This opens the Insert Citation menu, shown in Figure 15.10.

Figure 15.10
Use the Insert Citation menu to create a documented source for the information contained in your document.

3 Click **Add New Source**. This displays the Create Source dialogue box shown in Figure 15.11. Note: If you click Add a Placeholder, a question mark appears next to the placeholder in the Source Manager as a reminder to fill in the source information at a later time.

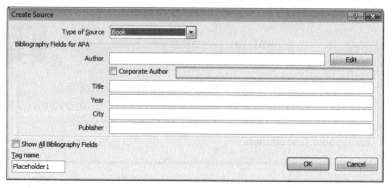

Figure 15.11
The Create Source dialogue box displays only the required fields, by default. You can display more fields of information by clicking the checkbox next to Show All Bibliography Fields.

4 Fill in the source information.

5 Click **OK**. This adds your citation to the document at the cursor location. You can see a sample website cited in Figure 15.12.

Adding Endnotes and Footnotes

Footnotes[1] and Endnotes are often used by people writing research papers to explain text references or document sources. (support.microsoft.com, 2007) Endnotes are references that print at the end of a document that explain text in a document; while, Footnotes are references that print at the bottom of each page and explain marked text located on the same page.

Figure 15.12
Citations are inserted inline with document text. When you click a citation, you can click the dropdown arrow that appears and choose to edit either the citation or the source.

Timesaver tip

Over time, your list of sources can begin to build. Word keeps track of your sources so that you can use them again. To see the sources you have already saved, click the Manage Sources command located in the Citations & Bibliography group on the Reference tab on the Ribbon. You'll notice that all of the citations you've ever used appear on the left, under Master List. To use previously created citations in a new document, select the desired citation under Master List and click Copy to copy the citation to the current document.

Now that you can create citations, let's take it one step further and look at how to generate a document's bibliography. To create a bibliography, all you need is one or more cited sources in a document. Once you've met this criterion, to generate a bibliography follow these steps:

1 Click at the end of the document. Note: Bibliographies can be inserted at any cursor position; however, they typically appear at the end of a document.

2 Click the **Bibliography** command located in the Citations & Bibliography group on the Reference tab on the Ribbon. This displays the Bibliography gallery shown in Figure 15.13.

3 Select a predefined bibliography format. (You can also choose Insert Bibliography to insert the bibliography information as plain text at the cursor location.)

15

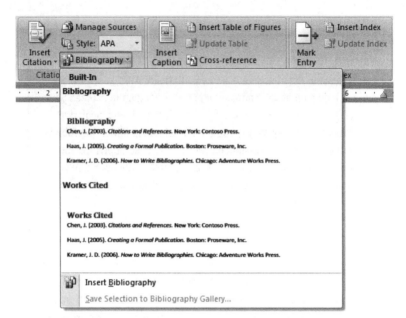

Figure 15.13
With the Bibliography gallery, you can choose from either of the
predefined bibliography formats or click "Insert Bibliography" to insert
a bibliography in plain text.

→ Summary

Footnotes, endnotes and the like are often a required part of
Word documents. With Word 2007's new Building Blocks, these
items are now less complicated in their use.

In the next chapter, you'll learn about using links in your Word
documents, including hyperlinks, bookmarks and cross-
references.

16

Using Links in Your Documents

In this new "Internet Age", many people use and follow hyperlinks every day – on the Internet. We click a link and quickly (well, quickly is a relative term based on the speed of your Internet connection) we "jump" to a new web page, document or a new e-mail window with the recipient's name already entered.

You can create similar links in your Word documents. Your Word links can jump you to a web page or other document. But, they can also jump you to specific places within the current document (known as a bookmark).

→ Adding Hyperlinks

If you've ever typed a website address in a Word document, you will already know that Word automatically converts any web address into an active hyperlink as soon as you type either a space or a hard return after the website address. Your newly typed text then becomes clickable text that typically appears as blue, underlined text. To avoid inadvertently jumping to a website while you're editing a document, Word forces you to press and hold Ctrl while clicking a hyperlink in a Word document before it will allow you to "jump" to the linked location.

Jargon buster

A **hyperlink** is clickable text (or a graphic) that generally appears as blue, underlined text. Each hyperlink "jumps" the reader to a new web page, document or pre-addressed e-mail.

There are actually several different types of hyperlinks you can create in a Word document. For example, you can create hyperlinks that jump to:

■ Websites

■ E-mail addresses

■ Other Word documents

■ Locations in the current Word document

■ New Word documents

Timesaver tip

Word 2007 automatically creates hyperlinks when you type a full web address in the document text followed by either a space or hard return.

We'll start by looking at creating a hyperlink that jumps the reader to either a web page or an existing document. These types of hyperlinks are beneficial for citing text or simply to refer people to specific sites. Many people opt to add a clickable hyperlink to their company's website at the bottom of each document page. To create a hyperlink to a web page or document, follow these steps:

1 Select the text (or graphic) the reader will click.

2 Click the **Hyperlink** command located in the Links group on the Insert tab on the Ribbon. This opens the Hyperlink dialogue box shown in Figure 16.1.

3 Under Link to, click **Existing File or Web Page**.

4 To link to a document, navigate to the document and select it. To link to a web page, type the entire web page address in the address box. Word may automatically add "http://" in front of any web page address you enter. This text is necessary for the hyperlink to work properly.

5 Click **OK**.

Figure 16.1
To link to a document or web page, under Link to, click Existing File or Web Page in the Hyperlink dialogue box.

Another idea for using hyperlinks is creating clickable e-mail addresses. This way, when a reader clicks the link, a new, pre-addressed e-mail message opens using the reader's default e-mail program. To create an e-mail hyperlink, follow these steps:

1 Select the text (or graphic) the reader will click.

2 Click the **Hyperlink** command located in the Links group on the Insert tab on the Ribbon. This opens the Hyperlink dialogue box shown in Figure 16.1.

3 Under Link to: click **E-Mail address**. This changes the Hyperlink dialogue box to reflect e-mail options as shown in Figure 16.2.

Figure 16.2
To link to an e-mail, under Link to: click E-mail address in the Hyperlink dialogue box. This action forces the Hyperlink dialogue box to display options specifically related to sending an e-mail.

4 Under E-mail address, enter the recipient's e-mail address. Note: Word will automatically add "mailto:" in front of any e-mail address you enter. This text is necessary for the hyperlink to work properly.

5 Click **OK**.

Timesaver tip

Typically, when you rest their mouse over a hyperlink, a ScreenTip displays with the e-mail address (or web page, etc.) indicating where the link refers to. However, you can customise the ScreenTip that appears. In the Hyperlink dialogue box, click the ScreenTip button. This opens the ScreenTip dialogue box. In this box, type the text you want to appear as the ScreenTip and click OK.

If you have used the default heading styles (Heading 1, Heading 2 or Heading 3) anywhere in your document, you can use the Hyperlink command to link to those areas as well. To create a

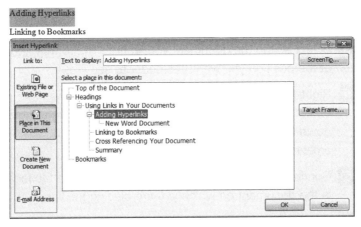

Figure 16.3
To link to a place within the document, under Link to, click Place in This Document in the Hyperlink dialogue box. This action forces the Hyperlink dialogue box to display all text formatting with a Heading style.

hyperlink to link to a specific location within the current document, follow these steps:

1 Select the text (or graphic) the reader will click.

2 Click the **Hyperlink** command located in the Links group on the Insert tab on the Ribbon. This opens the Hyperlink dialogue box shown in Figure 16.1.

3 Under Link to, click **Place in This document**. This changes the Hyperlink dialogue box to reflect Heading options as shown in Figure 16.3.

4 Select the heading to which you want to link.

5 Click **OK**.

To quickly create a hyperlink to an existing open document, you can drag a portion of the document text (using the right mouse button) from one document to the other. When you drag text with the right mouse button, a shortcut menu opens when you release the mouse button, giving you the option of creating a hyperlink. To create a hyperlink using drag and drop, follow these steps:

1 Open the document you want the hyperlink in.

2 Open the document you want to link to.

3 Select text in the document you want to link to that appears at the position you want the reader to see first.

4 Right-drag the selected text to the other document's button on the Taskbar and then pause (while continuing to hold down the right mouse button). The document you are creating the hyperlink in will open.

5 Continue to drag with the right mouse button to the location in the document on which you are placing the link.

6 Release the right mouse button. This displays the shortcut menu shown in Figure 16.4.

7 Choose **Create Hyperlink Here**. This creates in one document a hyperlink to the original document text.

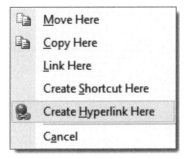

Figure 16.4
Using drag and drop to generate this handy shortcut menu, you can
quickly create hyperlinks between two open documents.

→ Linking to Bookmarks

In order to create links within the current document without using
the Heading styles, you'll need to use bookmarks. A bookmark
identifies a selection of text that you can quickly jump to or use
for future reference. Interestingly enough, hyperlinks between
web pages that jump to specific areas on a page are also called
bookmarks.

Jargon buster
A **bookmark** identifies a selection of text that you can quickly jump to
or use for future reference.

To add a bookmark, follow these steps:

1 Select the text you want to bookmark.

2 Click the **Bookmark** command located in the Links group on
the Insert tab on the Ribbon. This opens the Bookmark
dialogue box, shown in Figure 16.5.

3 Enter a bookmark name.

4 Click **Add**.

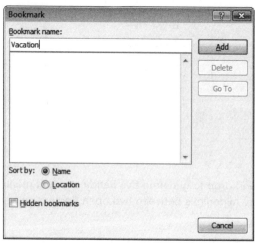

Figure 16.5
Click the Bookmark command located in the Links group on the Insert tab to enter, delete or navigate to a bookmark in the current document.

Important

Bookmark names cannot contain spaces and they must start with a letter.

Once you've created bookmarks, you can use the link to Place in This Document option in the Hyperlink dialogue box to generate hyperlinks to bookmarked text. To create a hyperlink to bookmarked text, follow these steps:

1 Select the text (or graphic) the reader will click.

2 Click the **Hyperlink** command located in the Links group on the Insert tab on the Ribbon. This opens the Hyperlink dialogue box, shown in Figure 16.1.

3 Under Link to, click **Place in This document**. This changes the Hyperlink dialogue box to reflect heading options as shown in Figure 16.6.

4 Select the bookmark to which you want to link.

5 Click **OK**.

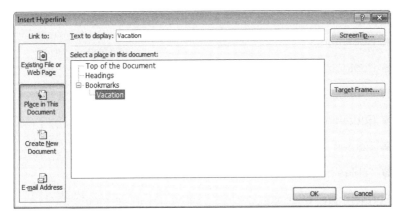

Figure 16.6
To link to a bookmark within the document, under Link to, click Place in This Document in the Hyperlink dialogue box. Then, under the Bookmark heading, choose the Bookmark to which you are linking.

Timesaver tip

You can quickly edit bookmarks in your document – that is, if you can see them. By default, bookmarks are not displayed, not even when you display non-printing characters. However, by modifying your Word options, you can see all of the bookmarks in the document. Open the Office Menu and choose Word Options. Next, click the Advanced category and then click the checkbox next to Show Bookmarks. Finally, click OK and voilà! – you can now see your bookmarks.

16

→ Cross-referencing Your Document

When hyperlinks and bookmarks don't give you all the linking options you need, take a good look at creating cross-references. With cross-references, you have a level of access to linking to things in your document that you may not have seen before.

With cross-references, you can create references to the following document items:

■ Numbered items

- Headings
- Bookmarks
- Footnotes
- Endnotes
- Equations
- Figures
- Tables

Furthermore, once you decide what you want to create a reference to, you can choose whether you want to reference the text, page number or heading number. To insert a cross-reference in your document, follow these steps:

1 Position the cursor at the location of the new cross-reference.

2 Click the **Cross-reference** command located in the Links group on the Insert tab on the Ribbon. This opens the Cross-reference dialogue box shown in Figure 16.7.

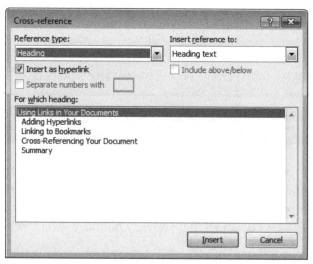

Figure 16.7
Use the Cross-reference dialogue box to create custom references to various parts of your document.

3 Click the dropdown arrow next to **reference type**. This displays the available document parts to which you can reference, as shown in Figure 16.8. Choose your desired reference type.

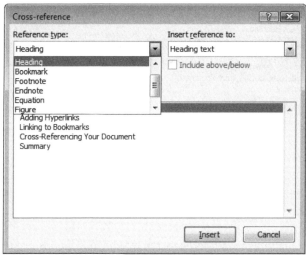

Figure 16.8
When creating a cross-reference, the reference types are many and varied and include items such as headings, bookmarks and footnotes.

4 Click the dropdown arrow next to **Insert reference** to. This displays the available locations to which you can reference, as shown in Figure 16.9. Choose your desired reference type.

5 Click the appropriate reference in the text box.

6 Click **OK**.

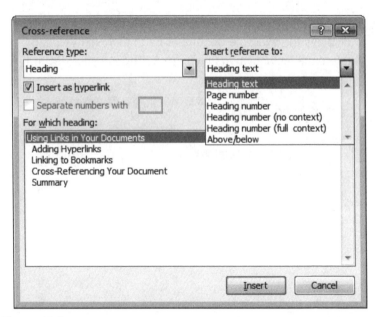

Figure 16.9
When creating a cross-reference, the reference locations include such places as page number, heading text and heading number.

→ Summary

With hyperlinks, you can add a level of functionality to your documents with which many people are already familiar from their experience working with the Internet.

In the next chapter, you'll learn everything you need to know about mail merge. From working with variable data to preparing the final merged document and everything in between, you'll go through all of the steps involved in creating a successful mail merge.

17

Creating Mass Mailings

Maintaining communication with your contacts is a critical component of staying in business. One Word 2007 tool you can use to keep in contact is the mail merge feature. With mail merge you can quickly print (or e-mail) letters addressed to all of your contacts.

Since Word is a Microsoft product it plays really well with its siblings: Outlook, Excel and Access. This means you can use Word to create the letter (or the e-mail) and then use an already created contact list stored in any of those other programs.

→ Understanding Mail Merge

Mail merge is the process of combining a set of variable data with a set of static (or boilerplate) text. For example, all customers in a business may need to receive an update on the business billing practices. In this scenario, you want each customer to think the letter they receive is personally meant for them. To achieve this result, you could use mail merge to create a boilerplate letter that includes a custom salutation for each customer.

Jargon buster

Mail merge is the process of combining a set of variable data with a set of static (or boilerplate) text.

Mail merge always consists of three files. They are:

- The mail merge data source
- The mail merge main document
- The final merged document

Let's look at each of these mail merge components.

The **mail merge data source** contains all the variable data that change from letter to letter (or e-mail to e-mail). Each data source consists of fields (or columns) of data (see Figure 17.1). Common entries in a mail merge data source include fields such as:

- First name
- Last name
- Address
- City
- County
- Postcode

First Name	Last Name	Adddress	City	State	Zip Code
Joe	Smith	123 Main Street	Anytown	VA	55555
Jim	Jones	123 Main Street	Anytown	VA	55555
Mary	Johnson	123 Main Street	Anytown	VA	55555
David	Reynolds	123 Main Street	Anytown	VA	55555
Sophia	Graham	123 Main Street	Anytown	CA	77777
Joe	Jones	123 Main Street	Anytown	CA	77777
Joey	Martin	123 Main Street	Anytown	CA	77777
Mary	Martin	123 Main Street	Anytown	CA	77777
Linda	Misher	123 Main Street	Anytown	MA	99999
Tina	Porter	123 Main Street	Anytown	MA	99999
Audra	Parker	123 Main Street	Anytown	MA	99999

Figure 17.1
Sample mail merge data source created in Microsoft Office Excel.

In addition to common fields, a mail merge data source can contain any fields that will change from letter to letter. For instance, you can send a letter to contributors thanking them for their recent donation. The general body of the letter for each contributor would remain the same but the contribution amount would differ from person to person. In a mail merge, you would add the contribution amount to the data source as this is information that would change from letter to letter.

Continuing with our contribution example, the text you want to send to every contributor goes inside the **mail merge main document** (see Figure 17.2). This is the second of your three mail merge files. Also included in the mail merge main document are links to the fields that change from letter to letter and point to the data contained in the data source.

17

The third mail merge file is the final **merged document**. This document is a result of the combination of the data source and the mail merge main document.

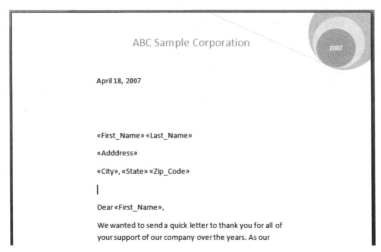

Figure 17.2
Sample mail merge main document created in Microsoft Office Word.

In Word 2007, you have the option of creating several different types of mail merge main documents. Available merged document types include:

- Letters

- E-mails

- Envelopes

- Labels

- Directories

With the new mail merge Ribbon, Word 2007 walks you through the mail merge process step by step.

→ Preparing Variable Data

Your variable data are the data stored in the data source. The variable data change from letter to letter (or from e-mail to e-mail) in the final merged document. Variable data can come from any number of sources, including:

- Microsoft Office Excel spreadsheet

- Microsoft Office Outlook contact list

- Microsoft Office Access table

- Microsoft Office Word table

- Any comma separated (.csv) file

Jargon buster

A **data source** is a separate file that contains the variable data that change from letter to letter in a mail merge. The data source is typically in a tabular or table format such as a Word or Access table or an Excel spreadsheet.

So that you can be sure that your variable data are set up properly, it's often most convenient to use either a tabular or a table structure. Programs like Excel and Access create this type of environment inherently. If you're using Microsoft Word, however, be sure to put your variable data inside a Word table. To connect it to an existing data source, follow these steps:

1 Click the **Select Recipients** command located in the Start Mail Merge group on the Mailings tab on the Ribbon. This displays the Select Recipients dropdown menu, as shown in Figure 17.3.

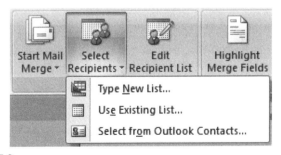

Figure 17.3
From the Select Recipients dropdown menu, choose Use Existing List to use variable data stored in a different file.

2 Click **Use Existing List**. This opens the Select Data Source dialogue box, shown in Figure 17.4.

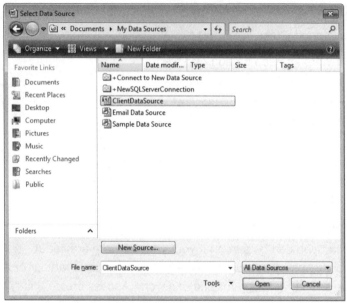

Figure 17.4
Once the Select Data Source dialogue box is displayed, navigate to the folder that contains the data source file.

3 Navigate to the folder that contains the data source file. Select the data source file and click **Open**. The selected data source is now attached to the document.

Microsoft Word's mail merge feature is also able to connect to an Outlook contact list. To do this follow these steps:

1 Click the **Select Recipients** command located in the Start Mail Merge group on the Mailings tab on the Ribbon. This displays the Select Recipients dropdown menu as shown in Figure 17.3.

2 Click **Select from Outlook Contacts**. This opens the Select Contacts dialogue box, shown in Figure 17.5.

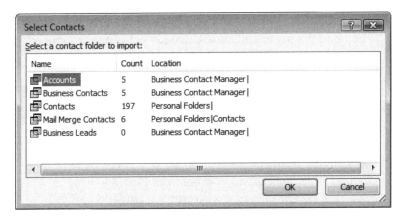

Figure 17.5
Using the Select Contacts dialogue box, you can choose from any individual contact list you have stored in Microsoft Office Outlook.

3 Select the name of the contact list you want to use and click **OK**. This displays the Mail Merge Recipients dialogue box, shown in Figure 17.6.

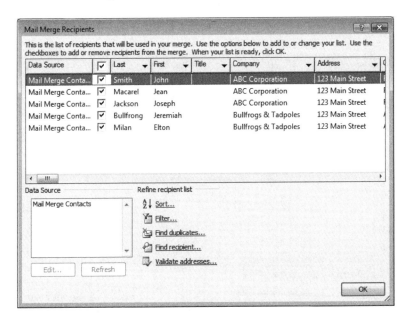

Figure 17.6
In the Mail Merge Recipients dialogue box, you can choose which contacts should receive your final, merged letter.

4 Click **OK**. This closes the Mail Merge Recipients dialogue box and the selected Outlook contact list is now attached to the document.

Timesaver tip

In any mail merge, you have total control over which contacts in the data source file receive the mailing. To select only specific contacts, click the Edit Recipient command located in the Start Mail Merge group. From the Edit Recipient dialogue box, you can select specific contacts to receive your mailing or click the Filter link to use only contacts that meet specific criteria.

Another option for creating variable data is to build it directly within the mail merge feature. This is a great option for when you don't have an existing variable data list already created in another program. To create a variable data source directly within the mail merge feature, follow these steps:

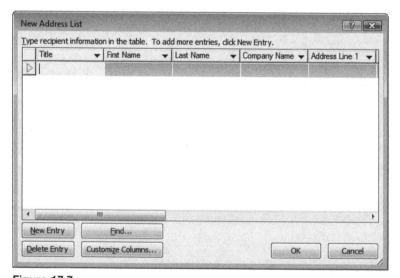

Figure 17.7
In the New Address List dialogue box, you can create a new data source on the spot.

1 Click the **Select Recipients** command located in the Start Mail Merge group on the Mailings tab on the Ribbon. This displays the Select Recipients dropdown menu, as shown in Figure 17.3.

2 Click **Type New List**. This opens the New Address List dialogue box shown in Figure 17.7.

3 Review the available fields (columns). If necessary, click the **Customize Columns** button. This opens the Customize Address List dialogue box shown in Figure 17.8. In this box, you can add, remove and reorder any columns to your new data list. Click OK when you've completed the column customisation.

Figure 17.8
Use the Customize Address List dialogue box (opened by clicking the Customize Columns button in the New Address List dialogue box) to add, remove and reorder the data list fields (columns).

4 Type one of the contacts for your data source and click **New Entry**. This adds a new line in the New Address List dialogue box.

5 Continue adding contacts, clicking **New Entry** after each addition.

6 Once all contacts have been added, click **OK**. This closes the New Address List dialogue box and the information is now attached to the document.

Timesaver tip

You can share your data sources with anyone. Because data sources can be stored as other file types, to share your data sources simply e-mail the source data. For instance, if your data source is contained in an Excel spreadsheet, e-mail your coworker the original Excel spreadsheet. This allows your coworker to use the same variable data with a different mail merge main document.

→ Preparing the Main Document

The mail merge main document contains the static information, or boilerplate text, that does not change from letter to letter. In order to set up your main document, you first need to determine what type of mail merge document you're creating.

Mail merge main documents can be:

- Letters
- E-mails
- Envelopes
- Labels
- Directories

Jargon buster

The **mail merge main document** contains the static information, or boilerplate text, that does not change from letter to letter.

To define your mail merge main document, follow these steps:

1 Click the **Start Mail Merge** command located in the Start Mail Merge group on the Mailings tab on the Ribbon. This opens the Start Mail Merge dropdown menu, as shown in Figure 17.9.

Figure 17.9
From the Start Mail Merge dropdown menu, you can choose which type of mail merge main document you need to create.

2 Click the option that defines the mail merge main document you are creating.

Important

Choosing Envelopes or Labels from the Start Mail Merge dropdown menu will launch related dialogue boxes. In each of these dialogue boxes, the most important step is choosing the size and layout of the paper to which you are printing.

Once you've defined your mail merge main document type, you're ready to enter the boilerplate text. This process is no more difficult than generating a regular Word document. All you really need to do is click inside your document and begin typing. You can use all of the regular Word features including tables, formatting, text boxes, Building Blocks and so on.

→ Inserting Merge Fields

After you've defined the variable data (data source) and the main document, you need to tell Word where to place the fields contained in the variable data file in the main document. You do this by inserting merge fields into the main document. This means, your main document will actually consist of static or boilerplate text and "links" to data contained in the data source. This way, you can use the mail merge main document and related data source over and over again.

Jargon buster

A **merge field** is a reference to a specific column in a data source file. Common merge fields include name, address and city.

To insert merge fields into your mail merge main document, follow these steps:

1 Position the cursor in the document.

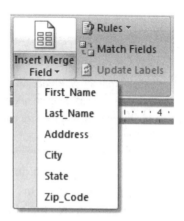

Figure 17.10
From the Insert Merge Field dropdown menu, you can select any of the fields contained in the attached data source to add to the mail merge main document.

2 Click the **Insert Merge Field** command located in the Write & Insert Fields group on the Mailings tab on the Ribbon. This displays the Insert Merge Field dropdown menu. An example is shown in Figure 17.10.

3 Click the field you want to insert into the document at the cursor location. The selected merge field is inserted into the document. You can see a sample set of inserted merge fields in Figure 17.11.

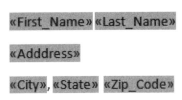

«First_Name» «Last_Name»

«Adddress»

«City», «State» «Zip_Code»

Figure 17.11
Inserted fields appear in the mail merge main document surrounded by << >>. Between and around merge fields, regular text can be entered.

→ Merging Documents

The final step in the mail merge process is to bring together the data source and the main document into one final, merged document. But, although it's the final step, there are actually several options. For example, you may want to send your document to only select people listed in your data source. You can filter your data source at this step (or at any step after you've selected the data source you will use). To filter the data source, follow these steps:

1 Click the **Edit Recipient List** command located in the Start Mail Merge group on the Mailing tab on the Ribbon. This opens the Mail Merge Recipients dialogue box shown in Figure 17.12.

2 Click the **Filter** link. This opens the Filter and Sort dialogue box, shown in Figure 17.13.

17

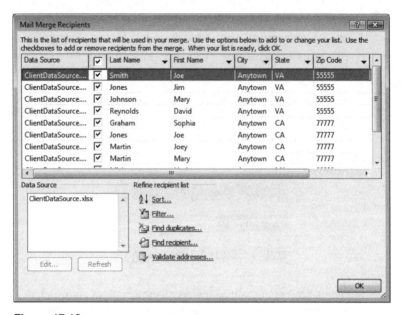

Figure 17.12
You can open the Mail Merge Recipients dialogue box by clicking the Edit Recipient List command located in the Start Mail Merge group.

3 In the first dropdown list, select the field you are filtering.

4 In the middle dropdown list, select the filter criteria.

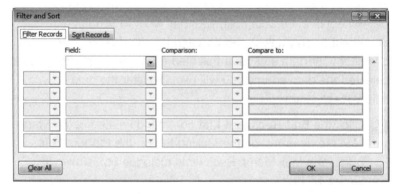

Figure 17.13
Use the Filter and Sort dialogue box to filter specific data source fields (columns) based on criteria you select.

5 In the last dropdown list, type the filter parameters.

6 For additional criteria sets, repeat Steps 3–5 in the remaining rows and then click **OK**. This closes the Filter and Sort dialogue box and returns the view to the Edit Recipient List dialogue box.

7 Click **OK** to close the Edit Recipient List dialogue box.

Once you've defined who is going to receive your letter and what the letter should look like, you're ready to either merge and print your letter or merge and e-mail your letter. But before you send the letters, be sure to preview the results. To preview a mail merge, follow these steps:

1 Click the **Preview Results** command located in the Preview Results group on the Mailings tab on the Ribbon. This updates the mail merge main document view to a view that displays the final, merged document.

2 Click the **Next** and **Previous** buttons in the Preview Results group to navigate through each of the letters.

3 When you've finished reviewing the merged letters, click the **Preview Results** command again to return to the mail merge main document view.

For Print

Before sending merged letters directly to the printer, make sure you preview the results following the previous set of steps. When you're ready to print the merged letters, follow these steps:

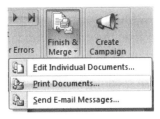

Figure 17.14
From the Finish & Merge dropdown menu, choose Print Documents to send the merged letters to the printer.

1 Click the **Finish & Merge** command located in the Finish group on the Mailings tab on the Ribbon. This displays the Finish & Merge dropdown menu, shown in Figure 17.14.

2 Click **Print Documents**. This displays the Merge to Printer dialogue box, shown in Figure 17.15.

Figure 17.15
When sending merged documents to the printer, you can choose to print all letters or only a specific range in the Merge to Printer dialogue box.

3 Set your merge options and click **OK**. This displays the Print dialogue box.

4 Click **OK**. This sends the merged letters to the printer.

For E-mail

Before sending merged letters through e-mail, be sure to preview the results following the previous set of steps. When you're ready to e-mail the merged letters, follow these steps:

1 Click the **Finish & Merge** command located in the Finish group on the Mailings tab on the Ribbon. This displays the Finish & Merge dropdown menu, shown in Figure 17.16.

2 Click **Send E-mail Messages**. This displays the Merge to E-mail dialogue box, shown in Figure 17.17.

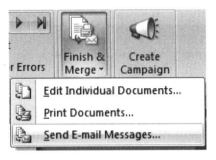

Figure 17.16
From the Finish & Merge dropdown menu, choose Send E-mail
Messages to send the merged letters through e-mail.

Figure 17.17
In the Merge to E-mail dialogue box, choose the data source field that
contains recipient e-mail addresses. You can also choose to e-mail all
letters or only a specific range.

3 Click the **To** dropdown arrow and choose the data source
field that contains recipient e-mail addresses.

4 Enter an e-mail subject in the **Subject** line box.

5 Set your merge options and click **OK**.

6 Click **OK**. This sends the merged letters directly to Outlook. If you're quick enough, you can open your Outbox folder and see the outgoing messages. An example is shown in Figure 17.18.

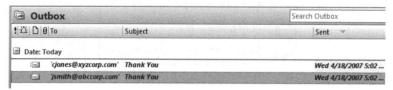

🗔 **Outbox**		Search Outbox	
! 🗓 🗅 📎 To	Subject	Sent ▼	
🖃 Date: Today			
📧 'cjones@xyzcorp.com'	Thank You	Wed 4/18/2007 5:02 ...	
📧 'jsmith@abccorp.com'	Thank You	Wed 4/18/2007 5:02 ...	

Figure 17.18
Outgoing merged e-mail messages briefly display in the Outlook Outbox before they are sent on.

Important

Another item worth mentioning in the Finish & Merge menu is the option to Edit Individual Documents. When you select this option, Word creates a new document out of the selected data source and main document. This provides a separate merged file that you can either review again or save for later use.

→ Creating Envelopes and Mailing Labels

You already know how to select envelopes or labels as your mail merge main document type. In this lesson you'll learn how to create individual envelopes or labels using their respective commands on the Ribbon. These commands (shown in

Figure 17.19
You can use the Envelopes and Labels commands on the Mailings tab to print individual envelopes or labels.

Figure 17.19), although located on the Mailings tab, are slightly outside of the mail merge process.

There are times when you need to type just a single envelope or maybe you need just a few mailing labels. For small tasks like these, it's faster to use the individual envelopes and mailing labels commands as opposed to setting up an entire mail merge.

To create an envelope in a new document, follow these steps:

1 Click the **Envelopes** command located in the Create group on the Mailings tab on the Ribbon. This displays the Envelopes and Labels dialogue box, shown in Figure 17.20.

Figure 17.20
You can use the Envelopes and Labels dialogue box to add return and delivery address information.

2 Add the envelope return address and delivery address.

3 Click the **Envelope Options** button. This opens the Envelope Options dialogue box, shown in Figure 17.21.

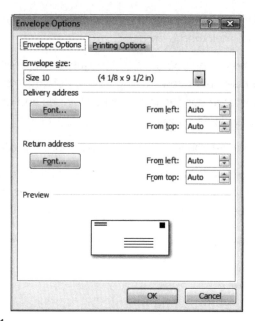

Figure 17.21
You can use the Envelope Options dialogue box to set the envelope size as well as the return and delivery address fonts.

4 Set the envelope size and address fonts and click **OK**.

5 In the Envelopes and Labels dialogue box, click either **Print** or **Add to Document**.

To create a mailing label, follow these steps:

1 Click the **Labels** command located in the Create group on the Mailings tab on the Ribbon. This displays the Envelopes and Labels dialogue box, shown in Figure 17.22.

2 Enter the information for the single label in the top box.

3 Click the **Options** button. This opens the Label Options dialogue box, shown in Figure 17.23.

Figure 17.22
You can use the Envelopes and Labels dialogue box to define labels, including creating one page of the same label or printing one label at a specific position on the label page.

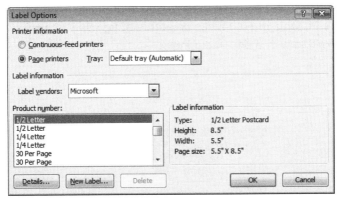

Figure 17.23
You can use the Label Options dialogue box to set the label size.

4 Select the label and click **OK**.

5 In the Envelopes and Labels dialogue box, click either **Print** or **New Document**.

Timesaver tip

To create a full page that acts as a label template, click the Labels command and then click the Options button. Once in the Label options dialogue box, select the label you typically print on and click OK. Now simply click New Document in the Envelopes and Labels dialogue box. This creates a new Word document with a table laid out precisely to your label specifications. On this blank document, you can now enter individual labels in each table cell.

→ Summary

Knowing how to piece together a mail merge is an advanced skill that will save you time in the future.

In the next chapter, you'll learn about one of the areas that people need help on the most – working effectively with long documents. In addition to working with section breaks, you'll learn how to create three different types of tables – table of contents, table of authorities and table of figures – as well as tips for working with a document index.

18

Working Effectively with Long Documents

Once word gets around that you know how to do a few cool things in Word, before you know it people will be looking to you to customise their documents. One of the areas that people need help with the most seems to be working effectively with long documents.

Many people can create a 50-page document with different headers and footers on the first page, odd and even pages. But when you ask them to create different headers and footers for different parts of the document they run into a roadblock. This is just one of the things that you'll learn how to do in this chapter as you find out about sections.

→ Adding Document Sections

Adding a section break is similar to adding a page break. The difference is that when you add a page break, the page margins remain the same throughout the document. But when you add a section break, you suddenly have the option of assigning different page margins to each page in your document.

Jargon buster

A **section** in a document is a page or set of pages that contains formatting which is different from the other pages in the document. Sections are defined by using section breaks.

Jargon buster

A **section break** creates division lines between sections in a document. Section breaks can be continuous, next page, odd page and even page.

For example, let's look at the typical three-page document shown in Figure 18.1.

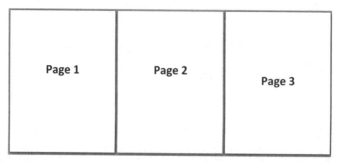

Figure 18.1
This figure shows a typical three-page document layout.

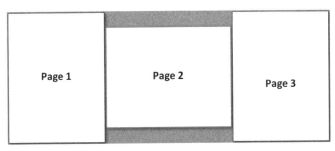

Figure 18.2
This figure shows a three-page document layout, with one page in landscape orientation.

With section breaks, you can take this sample document and display page 2 as landscape, as shown in Figure 18.2.

To achieve this layout, you need to divide your document into three sections. You can accomplish this by creating a Next Page Section Break at the end of page 1 and another Next Page Section Break at the end of page 2. This creates a document with three sections. Each section in the document can have its own page layout defined. This is what allows you to then apply landscape formatting to page 2, as shown in Figure 18.2.

There are four different types of section breaks:

- **Next Page** – creates a break very similar to a regular page break whereas the next page is based on the current page.

- **Continuous** – creates a break that allows for different formatting within the same page. For example, columns use a continuous section break before and after the column formatting.

- **Odd page** – creates a break that forces the next page to always fall on an odd number.

- **Even page** – creates a break that forces the next page to always fall on an even number.

To insert a section break, follow these steps:

1 Click in the document where you want the section break.

18

2 Click the **Breaks** command in the Page Setup group on the Page Layout tab on the Ribbon. This displays the Breaks menu, as shown in Figure 18.3.

3 Choose the section break that best suits your current document needs from the Breaks menu.

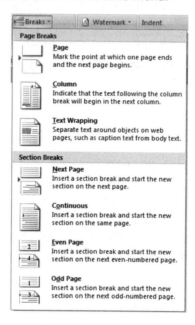

Figure 18.3
There are several options listed in the Breaks menu. Select the type of section break that best suits your current document needs.

To delete a section break, follow these steps:

1 Click at the beginning of the manual section break.

2 Press **Delete** on the keyboard. This deletes the section break.

Timesaver tip

You can view section breaks by clicking the Show/Hide command located in the Paragraph group on the Home tab.

→ Creating and Modifying a Table of Contents

A table of contents typically appears at or near the beginning of a long document and contains references to specific headings and subheadings based on applied styles.

Jargon buster

A **table of contents** typically appears near the beginning of a long document and contains references to specific headings and subheadings.

The first step to generating an accurate and automatic table of contents is to define the entries using styles. By default, Word 2007 refers to any text assigned the Heading 1, Heading 2 and Heading 3 styles as entries to be added to a table of contents. (Styles are covered in detail in Chapter 5.)

To generate a table of contents, follow these steps:

1 Assign Heading 1, Heading 2 and Heading 3 styles to any entries that should appear in the table of contents.

2 Position the cursor in the document at the location where the table of contents should begin.

3 Click the **Table of Contents** command located in the Table of Contents group on the References tab on the Ribbon. This displays the Table of Contents gallery, shown in Figure 18.4.

4 Choose one of the Table of Contents gallery objects.

If none of the table of contents gallery items suits your document needs, you can customise the table of contents you add to your document. To create a customised table of contents, follow these steps:

18

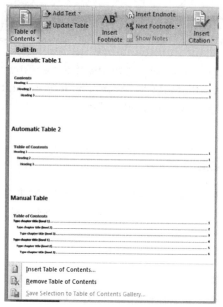

Figure 18.4
The Table of Contents dropdown menu provides a gallery of available predefined Building Blocks from which you can choose.

1 Assign Heading 1, Heading 2 and Heading 3 styles to any entries that should appear in the table of contents.

2 Position the cursor in the document at the location where the table of contents should begin.

3 Click the **Table of Contents** command located in the Table of Contents group on the References tab on the Ribbon. This displays the Table of Contents gallery, shown in Figure 18.4.

4 Click **Insert Table of Contents**. This displays the Table of Contents dialogue box, shown in Figure 18.5.

5 Set your table of contents preferences and click **OK**.

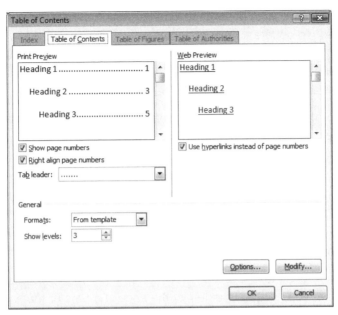

Figure 18.5
You can customise the format of a table of contents by choosing
Insert Table of Contents from the related gallery dropdown menu.

Timesaver tip

An existing table of contents does not update when the document text
changes. This means you could have a table of contents that points to
wrong page numbers. Whenever you make changes to your document,
make sure you update the table of contents as well. To update an
existing table of contents, simply click inside the table of contents (it
isn't necessary to highlight the entire table) and press F9 on the
keyboard.

There are several ways to modify the table of contents. First and
foremost is remembering to update the table of contents
whenever that document changes. If, after you create a table of
contents, you modify the document by adding pages or making
changes to the headings or the heading text, you need to update
the table of contents as well.

Updating the table of contents can be done from a few different places. To update a table of contents, first click inside the table. (It isn't necessary to highlight or select the entire table. Simply clicking inside the table is enough for this update procedure. You'll notice the entire table shades in grey.)

Once you've clicked inside the table of contents, choose one of the following methods to update the table.

■ Press **F9** on the keyboard.

■ Right-click the table and choose **Update Field** from the shortcut menu.

■ Click the **Update Table** command located in the Table of Contents group on the References tab on the Ribbon.

Using any of these methods may prompt a dialogue box asking whether you want to update just the page numbers or the entire table as shown in Figure 18.6. Choose your preferred option and click OK to update the table of contents.

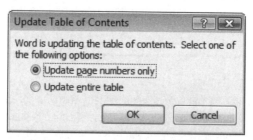

Figure 18.6
When updating a table of contents, you'll often be asked whether you want to update the page numbers only or the entire table.

Timesaver tip

Each table of contents contains a set of styles. For instance, the style TOC 1 refers to the display of all Heading 1 text in the document. TOC 2 and TOC 3 represent Heading 2 and Heading 3, respectively. You can modify the text formatting of the table of contents by modifying the related styles. (Styles are covered in detail in Chapter 5.)

Timesaver tip

To remove a table of contents from your document, you can either select the entire table and press delete on your keyboard or click the Table of Contents command and choose Remove Table from the menu.

→ Creating and Modifying an Index

An index typically appears at the end of a document, with references to specific text throughout the document.

Jargon buster

An index typically appears at the end of a document, with references to specific text throughout the document.

The first step in getting an index to generate automatically is to mark the index entries throughout the document. This often means going through your document line by line and marking individual entries.

When using this process, it's helpful to keep a list of the entries handy so that if the term appears on more than one page you're sure to name the index entry the same thing. To mark individual index entries, follow these steps:

1 Either select the term you want to mark or click immediately after the text.

2 Click the **Mark Index Entry** command located in the Index group on the References tab on the Ribbon. This opens the Mark Index Entry dialogue box, shown in Figure 18.7.

18

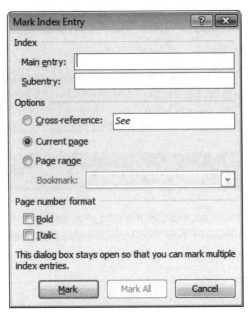

Figure 18.7
The Mark Index Entry dialogue box allows you to mark individual index entries.

3 In the Mark Index Entry dialogue box, complete the following sections:

- Main Entry (required): Enter the word(s) that will appear in the index alongside the page number, page range or cross-reference.

- Subentry (optional): Enter the word(s) that will appear in the index as a subentry to the main entry.

- Options (required): Choose one of the listed options.

4 Click **Mark**. This places the entry into the document at the cursor location.

5 The Mark Index Entry dialogue box remains open so you can continue to mark additional entries. Click **Cancel** once you've completed marking entries in the document.

Once entries have been marked throughout your document, you're then ready to insert the index. To insert an index, follow these steps:

1 Position the cursor in the document at the location where the index should begin.

2 Click the **Insert Index** command located in the Index group on the References tab on the Ribbon. This displays the Index dialogue box shown in Figure 18.8.

3 Select an index format.

4 Click **OK**. This closes the Index dialogue box and inserts an index at the cursor location.

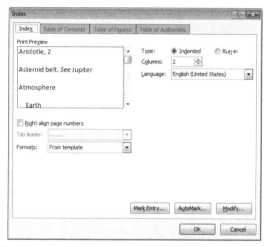

Figure 18.8
You can customise the format of an index in the Index dialogue box.

Timesaver tip

Inside the Index dialogue box, there's an added option to AutoMark your document. By using AutoMark, you eliminate the need to go through your document line by line, manually marking each entry. However, using the AutoMark feature requires you to have a separate saved document that contains a predefined list of the terms you want Word to mark.

If you make changes to your document after creating the index, you'll need to be sure to remember to update the index. Just as with updating a table of contents, there are several ways to update an index.

To update an index, first click inside the index. (It isn't necessary to highlight or select the entire index. Simply clicking inside the index is enough for this update procedure. You'll notice the entire index shades in grey.) Once you've clicked inside the index, choose one of the following methods to update the index.

- Press **F9** on the keyboard.

- Right-click the index and choose **Update Field** from the shortcut menu.

- Click the **Update Index** command located in the Index group on the References tab on the Ribbon.

Using any of these methods may prompt a dialogue box asking whether you want to update just the page numbers or the entire index. Choose your preferred option and click OK to update the index.

Timesaver tip

An existing index does not update when the document text changes. Whenever you make changes to your document, make sure you update the index as well. To update an existing index, simply click inside the index (it isn't necessary to highlight the entire index) and then press F9 on the keyboard.

→ Creating and Modifying a Table of Authorities

A table of authorities is typically used in legal documents to mark citations.

Just as creating an index requires you to mark individual index entries throughout your document, a table of authorities requires you to mark individual entries throughout your document as well. The difference is the table of authorities is typically used in a legal setting and with legal documents.

The entries that you mark for your table of authorities are actually citations. The first step to generating a table of authorities is marking the citations throughout your document. To mark citations, follow these steps:

1 Select the entry in the document you want to mark as a citation.

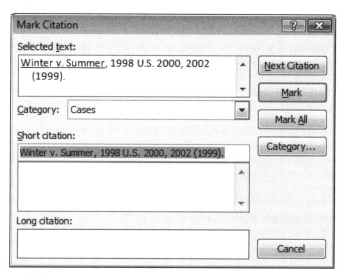

Figure 18.9
In the Mark Citation dialogue box, you'll notice the text that you selected and have the opportunity to select the type of citation you are marking.

2 Click the **Mark Citation** command located in the Table of Authorities group on the References tab on the Ribbon. This opens the Mark Citation dialogue box, shown in Figure 18.9.

3 In the Mark Citation dialogue box, complete the following sections:

- Category (required): Click the dropdown arrow and select the citation type, i.e. cases or statutes.

- Short Citation (optional): Edit the short citation text.

- Long Citation (optional): Edit the long citation text.

4 Click **Mark**. This places the entry into the document at the cursor location.

The Mark Citation dialogue box remains open so you can continue to mark additional citations. Click **Cancel** once you've completed marking citations in the document.

Once you've marked your citations, you're then ready to insert the table of authorities. To create a table of authorities, follow these steps:

1 Position the cursor in the document at the location where the table of authorities should begin.

2 Click the **Insert Table of Authorities** command located in the Table of Authorities group on the References tab on the Ribbon. This displays the Table of Authorities dialogue box, shown in Figure 18.10.

3 Select a Table of Authorities format.

4 Click **OK**. This closes the Table of Authorities dialogue box and inserts a table of authorities at the cursor location.

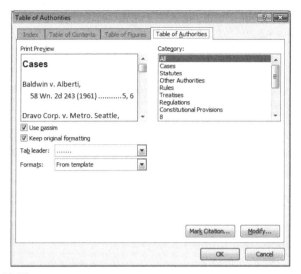

Figure 18.10
You can customise the format of a table of authorities in the Table of Authorities dialogue box.

Timesaver tip

If you don't see the citation entries in your document, click the Show/Hide button located in the Paragraph group on the Home tab on the Ribbon. When you display the citations, you can edit them simply by editing the text inside the citation. This is also how you delete a citation entry. Just make sure that you include all of the data inside the fancy brackets as well as the brackets when you press delete.

If you make changes to your citations after creating the table of authorities, you'll need to remember to update the table of authorities. Just as with updating a table of contents and the index, there are several ways to update a table of authorities. This can be done from a few different places.

To update a table of authorities, first click inside the table of authorities. (It isn't necessary to highlight or select the entire table of authorities. Simply clicking inside the table of authorities is enough for this update procedure. You'll notice the entire table of authorities shades in grey.) Once you've clicked inside the table of authorities, choose one of the following methods to update the table:

- Press **F9** on the keyboard.

- Right-click the table of authorities and choose **Update Field** from the shortcut menu.

- Click the **Update Table of Authorities** command located in the Table of Authorities group on the References tab on the Ribbon.

Timesaver tip

An existing table of authorities does not update when the document text changes. Whenever you make changes to your document, be sure to update the Table of Authorities as well. To update an existing table of authorities, simply click inside the table of authorities (it isn't necessary to highlight the entire table of authorities) and then press F9 on the keyboard.

→ Creating and Modifying a Table of Figures

A table of figures provides a listing of all marked figures in a document. Figures are marked with captions.

Jargon buster

A **table of figures** provides a listing of all marked figures in a document. Figures are marked with captions. Captions are covered in detail in Chapter 13.

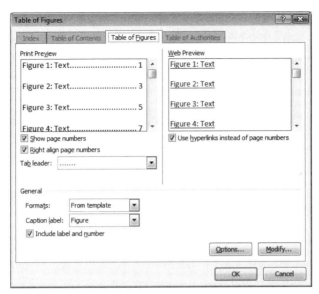

Figure 18.11
You can customise the format of a table of figures in the Table of Figures dialogue box.

With the table of contents, index and table of authorities features you had to do a little legwork up front before you could get Word to automatically generate your desired listing. The same is true for creating a table of figures.

Once the figures in a document are captioned, you're ready to generate a table of figures. To generate a table of figures, follow these steps:

1 Position the cursor in the document at the location where the table of figures should begin.

2 Click the **Table of Figures** command located in the Table of Figures group on the References tab on the Ribbon.
This displays the table of figures dialogue box, shown in Figure 18.11.

3 Select a table of figures format.

4 Click **OK**. This closes the Table of Figures dialogue box and inserts a table of figures at the cursor location.

If you add, remove or move captions after creating the table of figures, you'll need to remember to update the table of figures. Just as with updating a table of contents and the index, there are several ways to update a table of figures. This can be done from a few different places.

To update a table of figures, first click inside the table of figures. (It isn't necessary to highlight or select the entire table of figures. Simply clicking inside the table of figures is enough for this update procedure. You'll notice the entire table of figures shades in grey.) Once you've clicked inside the table of figures, choose one of the following methods to update the table:

- Press **F9** on the keyboard.

- Right-click the table of figures and choose **Update Field** from the shortcut menu.

- Click the **Update Table of Figures** command located in the Captions group on the References tab on the Ribbon.

Timesaver tip

An existing table of figures does not update when the document text changes. Whenever you make changes to your document, make sure you update the table of figures as well. To update an existing table of figures, simply click inside the table of figures (it isn't necessary to highlight the entire table) and then press F9 on the keyboard.

→ Summary

If you don't mind the small amount of legwork that needs to be done in order to use Word's table of figures, table of authorities, table of contents and index features, the rewards are definitely worth the time you put in.

In the next chapter, you'll learn about sending your documents to the printer as well as working with the available print settings.

19

Printing Your Documents

As much as we'd all like to move to a paperless society, that reality is probably further away than we'd like to think. In fact, many of us are still in the habit of printing every document just so that we have that hard-copy backup.

In this chapter you'll learn about the different options for sending your Word documents to the printer as well as changing your print settings.

→ Sending Your Documents to the Printer

When printing, you essentially have two options:

- Quick Print
- Print

If you choose the Quick Print option, your document is sent directly to the default printer without opening the Print dialogue box. To send a document directly to the printer, follow these steps:

1 Click the **Office button**. This opens the Office Menu.

2 Hover the mouse over the Print option. This displays the Print submenu shown in Figure 19.1.

3 Click **Quick Print**.

Figure 19.1
To send a document directly to the printer bypassing the Print dialogue box, select Quick Print from the Print submenu.

For more control over where your document prints, you can view
the print settings in the Print dialogue box before sending the
document to a printer. To print a document using the Print
dialogue box, follow these steps:

1 Click the **Office button**. This opens the Office Menu.

2 Hover the mouse over the Print option. This displays the
Print submenu shown in Figure 19.1.

3 Click **Print**. This opens the Print dialogue box shown in
Figure 19.2.

4 Click **Print**. This closes the Print dialogue box and sends the
active document to the printer.

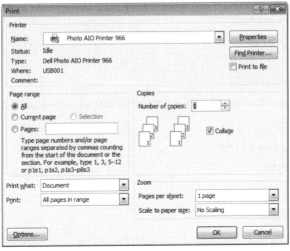

Figure 19.2
Use the Print dialogue box to modify print settings, including the
printer the document prints on and the number of copies that print,
among other options.

19

Timesaver tip

To quickly access the Print dialogue box, use the keyboard shortcut
combination Ctrl+P.

→ Changing Your Print Settings

To change your print settings, you need to access the Print dialogue box, shown in Figure 19.2.

Just choosing the Print command opens the Print dialogue box. Inside the Print dialogue box you can modify your print settings, including the printer you're sending the document to, the pages of the document you want to print and the number of copies that you want to print.

Print settings include:

- Printer
  - Properties
  - Find printer
- Page Range
  - All
  - Current page
  - Pages (separate non-contiguous pages with commas)
- Copies
  - Number of copies
  - Collate
- Zoom
- Pages per Sheet
- Scale to Paper Size

Additionally, you can choose to print just odd pages or just even pages in the document as well as printing other document information.

→ Previewing Your Print Job

Before you send a document to the printer, it's a good idea to view it in Print Preview. When you look at a document zoomed out in Print Preview, layout issues become clearer than when working in Print Layout view. To view a document in Print Preview, follow these steps:

1 Click the **Office button**. This opens the Office Menu.

2 Hover the mouse over the Print option. This displays the Print submenu shown in Figure 19.1.

3 Click **Print Preview**.

Timesaver tip

In Print Preview, if you see a small element of the document that needs correcting, you can quickly edit the document in Print Preview by removing the checkmark next to Magnifier in the Preview group.

In Print Preview, there are several options for viewing the document on the Print Preview tab shown in Figure 19.3.

Figure 19.3
The Print Preview tab on the Ribbon offers several choices for viewing and otherwise working with your document in Print Preview.

■ In the **Print** group, you can access the Print dialogue box and your default printer options.

■ In the **Page Setup** group, you can make changes to the page margins, orientation and size.

■ In the **Zoom** group, you can choose to zoom in or zoom out of the current view. To see more than two pages at a time, click the Zoom command.

■ In the **Preview** group, you can view the ruler, navigate between document pages in Print Preview and use the Shrink

One Page feature. This is also the group where you'll find the Close Print Preview command. Clicking this command closes Print Preview and returns you to your previous view.

→ Packaging Your Document for Outside Printing

Sending your document to an outside printer may be necessary not just in terms of quality but also for large numbers of copies. Occasionally, you may send a Word file that looks fine on your computer but may look slightly different on your printer's computer. Typically, that's due to either a lack of an appropriate print driver or a lack of specific fonts at the printer's end. This type of issue is rare, but it does happen. Another consideration is whether or not the final document will be bound (either on the left or at the top).

Word 2007 does have a couple of features that may help you avoid these issues when sending Word documents to an outside printing company.

Jargon buster

The **gutter** is the space between the edge of the paper and the related margin that allows for binding.

We'll look at the issue of binding first. Typically, when a document is printed and bound, the binding is located on the left side of the document; less frequently it is along the top edge. Word 2007 accounts for both of these scenarios with a gutter option. The gutter is the space between the edge of the paper and the related margin that allows for binding. To modify the gutter position, follow these steps:

1 Click the **dialogue box launcher arrow** located in the lower right corner of the Page Setup group located on the Page Layout tab on the Ribbon. This opens the Page Setup dialogue box, shown in Figure 19.4.

2 Set the **Gutter width** to an appropriate spacing based on the binding that will be used on the document.

3 Set the **Gutter location** to either Left or Top.

4 Click **OK**. This closes the Page Setup dialogue box.

Figure 19.4
Adjust the gutter width and location in the Page Setup dialogue box to account for any binding of the document after it has been printed.

For issues related to missing fonts or print drivers, Word 2007 offers the option of saving your Word documents to a fixed file format – such as a Portable Document Format (PDF). Saving documents as PDF files ensures they can't be changed en route to an outside printer.

19

Important

At the time of writing, the Save to PDF option doesn't install automatically with Word 2007. However, there is a free download available on the Microsoft website at www.Microsoft.com (from the Home Page, conduct a search using the term "Word 2007 Save As PDF"). Once this is downloaded, you'll be able to save your Word documents in the PDF format.

In fact, many commercial printers prefer to receive custom print jobs in a PDF format. To save a Word document as a PDF file, follow these steps:

1 Click the **Office button**. This opens the Office Menu.

2 Hover the mouse over the Save As option. This displays the Save As submenu, shown in Figure 19.5.

Figure 19.5
Choose Save As PDF or XPS to save your Word document in the PDF format. Remember, you may need to download Microsoft's free add-in for this feature to work properly.

3 Click **PDF or XPS** on the Save As submenu. This displays the Publish as PDF or XPS dialogue box, shown in Figure 19.6.

Figure 19.6
By choosing PDF or XPS, the Publish as PDF or XPS dialogue box automatically opens. Verify that the Save As type reflects "PDF".

4 Verify that the Save as type reflects "PDF".

5 Enter a file name.

6 (optional) Click **Options**. This opens the PDF Options dialogue box, shown in Figure 19.7.

7 Define the PDF save options as they pertain to your document and then click **OK**. This closes the PDF Options dialogue box.

8 Click **Publish**. This generates a PDF file of the document and in most cases launches your default PDF reader with the new PDF document.

19

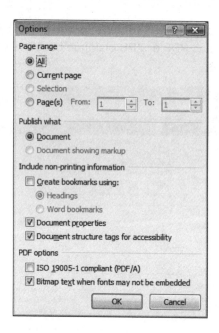

Figure 19.7
The PDF options you choose will ultimately depend on the final document output. This box gives you some of the same options that you would see in the Print dialogue box.

→ Summary

While we may still be years away from a paperless office, with the options available in the Print dialogue box at least you can be a little pickier over which document pages you choose to print.

In the next chapter, you'll learn all about creating Word documents that can be published to the web.

20

Creating Documents for the Web

Many of us would like to say that we're web designers, but the reality is that we're probably pretty far away from having that level of knowledge. However, with Word 2007, we can create some fairly slick static web pages. Of course, you'll still need to talk to those people who consider themselves web designers to get your pages uploaded to the Internet.

→ Creating a Web Document

Believe it or not, creating a web document in Word isn't much more difficult than choosing a web page file type in the Save As dialogue box (shown in Figure 20.1). When you save a Word document as a web page, Word adds the file extension .mht.

Figure 20.1
To create a web page using Microsoft Word 2007, simply choose web page as the file type when saving the document.

To create a web document, follow these steps:

1 Create the Word document, as you would normally.

2 Click the **Office** button. This opens the Office Menu.

3 Click **Save As**. This opens the Save As dialogue box, shown in Figure 20.1.

4 Click the dropdown arrow next to Save as type and choose **Single File Web Page** from the list. This updates the Save

As dialogue box to include the Change Title button, as shown in Figure 20.2.

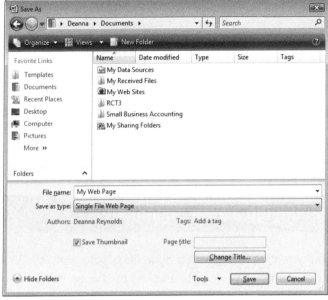

Figure 20.2
Once you select Single File Web Page from the Save as type dropdown list, the Save As dialogue box updates to include a Change Title button.

5 (optional) Click the **Change Title** button. This opens the Change Title dialogue box, shown in Figure 20.3. Enter a title for the web page and click OK.

6 Click **Save**. The document is saved as a web page and the document view is changed to Web Layout.

Timesaver tip

To see what your Word document would look like as a web page, you can switch to Web Layout view at any time by clicking the Web Layout view icon next to the Zoom Slider located in the lower right corner of the Word window.

Figure 20.3
The title of a web page appears in the Internet browser title bar when a reader opens the web page. Common titles including company names and/or taglines.

→ Modifying a Web Document

Although creating a single web page file is fairly simple in Word, there may be times when you're asked to change some more advanced web page settings. It's important to remember that Word is a document-editing program, not a web-design program. As such, it's web-editing options are somewhat limited.

However, from the Save As dialogue box, you do have access to a few web-based save options, as shown in Figure 20.4.

To access the Web Options dialogue box, follow these steps:

1 From the open web page, click the **Office** button. This opens the Office Menu.

2 Click **Save As**. This opens the Save As dialogue box shown in Figure 20.1. Even if the document already has a name, you need to access the Save As dialogue box for the next step.

3 Click the **Tools** button. This opens the Tools menu shown in Figure 20.4.

4 Click **Web Options**. This opens the Web Options dialogue box, shown in Figure 20.5.

Figure 20.4
Although Word is not designed to do heavy web page editing, you do have access to a few web setting defaults by clicking the Tools menu in the Save As dialogue box.

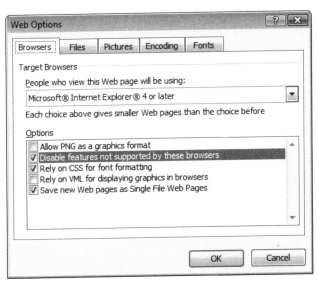

Figure 20.5
From the Tools menu, choose Web Options to open the Web Options dialogue box. In this dialogue box, you can set web options relative to the web page you are creating.

20

5 Set specific web options relative to the web page you are creating and click **OK**.

5 Click **Save**. Word will then prompt you to overwrite the existing file.

→ Summary

Although Word does have the functionality to save documents as web pages, the program is not a web page designer. As a result, you can really only create static, information-based web pages. And without access to uploading options, you'll need to check with your website experts on the best way to get your web pages on the web server.

brilliant
pocket books

ONLY
£8.99

The ultimate pocket sized guides to the new Windows Vista and Office 2007

brilliant pocket books – the fast answer